Diamonds AND *Curlz*™

29 YEARS ROLLING WITH ROCK ROYALTY

PRINCE

BY

KIM BERRY

WITH ANDREA WILLIAMS

DIAMONDS AND CURLZ:
29 Years Rolling With
Rock Royalty
PRINCE

Volume 1

Copyright © 2019 Kim Berry

Visit our Web site at www.diamondsncurlz.com

(Paperback) ISBN: 9781090531353

Printed in the United States of America

First Edition

Xtralovable

Just as
Donald and Joanna Berry
Begat
The Diamond, Kim Berry

Prince always said, " You know your children are you in the future?"

Well, here's 2 U
Sieara DeLone
a.k.a.
"Sisi the Lyricist"

Because she is Woman
Author, Singer, Songwriter, Actress, Spoken Word Artist, Activist, and Change Agent

I'm so glad she chose me
2 come unto life
To B
A Beautiful reflection of God's grace.

Somewhere Here on Earth

BEAUTIFUL, LOVED AND BLESSED

KIM BERRY... TWO WORDS.

I F THERE WERE a Webster's definition behind Kim's name, it would read: "Realest, fiercest hairstylist full of honesty and style."

When I first met Kim, she treated me as if I was her little sister, and not just because we are both women of color. Kim's sisterly instincts are natural and effortless, just like the "Hey, girlfriend, how are you?" she still greets me with. And upon meeting her, I immediately understood why Prince, the greatest legend of all time, took a true liking to her for nearly three decades.

Kim may be a hairstylist, but she's also a woman of integrity. When you sit in her chair—whether voluntarily or by invitation—and share your vision, she brings it to life, elevating your initial idea to perfection without ever seeking your approval along the way. And don't be fooled: She knows how to hold her own. Kim Berry truly understands when to be a "yes" woman—and when to be a "no" woman when the time comes.

Hairstylists are all around us, but it takes true humility and grit to hang in the game, silently maneuvering with artists such as Prince. A mother and powerful energy to connect with in any room, Kim is candid; she is frank; she is love.

1

Kim's story is impactful, and because it lacks the typical industry gossip and slander, it provides a true behind-the-scenes look at what it takes to operate at the top of your game while being in the presence of an icon that always operated at the top of his.

Kim knows her gift, and without the need to show and prove, she exudes excellence. If you are ever in need of someone to help you define your own beauty, I have only two words: KIM BERRY.

Ashley Tamar Davis, Singer/Songwriter/Philanthropist

Kim Berry is nobility at its best. She has the bold confidence of a Master of Her Craft who's been around the word twice and the humble spirit and gentle nature of an apprentice on the first day of training. A risk taker willing to take a chance on something new, but sensible enough to hold fast to the tried and true. A perpetual student of her craft and an ever-ready teacher to all who desire to learn. Kim is a positive light, and a creative force. Her talent is next level amazing and is only surpassed by her selfless, caring nature, willingness to give back and consistent support of fellow artists in our industry. She is a superstar. I'm sure that Prince was aware of how blessed and lucky he was to have her on his team.

Mann Nance, Celebrity Hair/Makeup Artist

30 years ago I remember cutting my hair at the age of 15. My mother, also a hairstylist, would say hair is a growing business. I remember my high school friends called me Anita Baker, but oh my when Prince pictures of his short hairstyle appeared in magazines and on TV, I was such a fan and loved his hair.

As a makeup artist for 20 years, who would've thought

that I would have the pleasure of meeting and working with Kim. She not only hired me to make her daughter day the most memorable but as I was packing up my makeup kit, I remember her saying something like this; hey sis we're going to work together on future projects. She kept her word and called shortly after for a video shoot and that was the start of our friendship.

Kim Berry please continue to pave the way for other Beauty Professionals. We need you. I'm extremely proud of you.

Ann Mosley, Celebrity Makeup Artist

Prince has always been the Artist of our time to me. Who best reflects life and creativity but My Girl Kim B. Kim was a part of this magical crown. Flavor with a God flow.

Prince said, "Despite everything, no one can dictate who you are to other people."[1] People will always have their opinions. Only you know who you really are. Focus on living authentically and honestly, have integrity in all that you do and those opinions won't matter. "A strong spirit transcends rules."[2] People who have no creativity, talent or courage are the ones who follow the rules. Be brave, be bold, step up and make your own! The passion that lies inside of you doesn't need to follow the pack because you transcend it.

Kim B. has been a trendsetter for so many years and we always looked forward to what Prince was going to do next.

I knew at a very young age it was just fine to be FREE & ME.

Yolande' Denise, Celebrity Makeup Artist

REVELATION

Deciding how to write about Prince wasn't easy, namely because of his powerful legacy. He was one of the greatest artists of our time, an innovator who lived to shatter the status quo and did so every chance he got. Whether it was with his wardrobe and hair, the music he created, or the independent business empire he built, he was determined to go against the grain.

After spending nearly three decades with Prince as his trusted hairstylist and friend, I could only respect his ground-breaking approach to art and commerce. When it came time for me to sit down to write this story—one that covers the ups and downs of my life with Prince, while revealing a human, and yet unseen, side of him—I wanted to take a similarly unique approach.

I could have written one long book, ordered chronologically and broken into numbered chapters. But if I learned nothing else from my 29 years with Prince, it's that doing what everyone else does is boring and, often, ineffective.

So I decided to take a different approach. Because Prince was truly a rare gem, the likes of whom we'll probably never see again, and because I wanted to honor his multiplatinum album *Diamonds and Pearls*, I have structured my story around the five "C"s of a diamond. The five Cs are the characteristics that determine the value and beauty of a diamond, and they are also the perfect instruments to illustrate the value and beauty of Prince himself.

As we start, I invite you to play your favorite Prince jams, light a purple candle, and enjoy. I want you to know that, whether you rocked with Prince for every one of his 39 studio albums, or you just popped in and out of his catalog at the point of his biggest, chart-topping hits, he loved you, and was honored to have you as a fan.

Today, I am honored to share our story with you.

I WEEP 4 U

I weep 4 U...
4 every lie
They told on U
After all
U contributed
2 the world at large

4 every drop of energy
U gave on the stage
Daily, yearly
Never asking
4 anything in return
But 4 the crowd to simply
ENJOY THEMSELVES
And
BE PRESENT N THE MOMENT

4 every time we talked about
The government
Mistreating the people of the world
And what could we do
In our own communities
2 make a difference

4 every person
U had to pay
2 be around your genius
(Your "Frenemies")

4 every song
U had yet to write
Every stage
U had yet to rock
4 simply wanting
2 be NORMAL
To get an iced coffee
Or a cheese on a stick in the mall

4 never seeing your son
Amir grow up

My heart is broken
But I can rejoice
Through the sorrow
Through the sorrow
Knowing that U...
Are Now FREE!!!

Praise God U ARE FREE
We discussed time travel on end
Atoms moving faster than light
TRANSPORTING us
2 faraway lands
Transcending time and space

Now U've made
The ULTIMATE TRANSITION

U are now…
Like the Creator
"EVERYWHERE "
Your music lives on forever

Everyone loved your beauty
Your impeccable style and swagger
For every monument
Around the globe
The Day the world
Turned purple
The images from
The four corners
Of the Earth
Circulating daily
Remind me of the good times…
Of every memory
From every moment
U existed

I smile
As the memories play back in my mind
That God allowed for me

Joanna's Daughter
Sieara's mom, as U called Me
This lil' girl from the hood
Did good!

2 tell the story
Of how we moved across
Nations
Presenting your greatness
2 the masses
In methods like no other had or will…
EVER

So rock on with your BAD SELF!!
My brother and my friend
Even after your sudden and tragic
Departure

N2 the purple rain U strutted
The doves cried
And THE BAND ... PLAYED ON

Tribute after tribute
Like a shooting star
Streaking across the sky
SO GLAD WE HAD THE REAL THANG BABY

See U at the exchange desk
Prince
Where we will exchange
Our Cross
For our crown

Kim Berry

SOMETIMES IT SNOWS IN APRIL

ASK ANY PRINCE fan where he, or she, was when they heard about his death, and they can surely tell you. She may have been at the grocery store picking up food for dinner, or maybe he was at the gym, or picking up dry cleaning. Without fail, they can all remember the exact moment they learned that the world had lost the Purple One.

Me? I was driving down the street when John, a hairstylist friend, called. I immediately noticed his uneven breathing, the cracks in his voice.

"Have you seen the news?" he said.

"Seen the news? No, I haven't. Why?"

John paused, took a deep breath. "What are you doing?"

"I'm driving. Why?" I was getting anxious, wondering why he wouldn't just tell me whatever was obviously bothering him.

"Kim, I need you to pull over."

My anxiety had been replaced by absolute fear. I gripped the steering wheel tightly, checked the rearview mirror and eased into the parking lot of a nearby barbershop. "Okay, John. I pulled over. Now you need to tell me what the hell is going on!"

He told me to pull up the TMZ website. After some hesitation (I don't pay much attention to gossip sites), I landed on the homepage. The feature story's headline was big and bold.

13

A blaring announcement! There had been a fatality at Paisley Park, Prince's creative compound in Chanhassen, Minnesota.

"That could be anybody," I said as my heart rate started to gather speed. "Maybe it was some female who was visiting—"

I could barely get the words out when my phone beeped, alerting me to an incoming call. It was another friend, Rodney, who was a cameraman working for CBS. I told John to hold and pushed the answer button.

"Kim." Rodney said immediately, "We're going live in 5 minutes. I just wanted you to know."

I didn't realize it at the time, but those were the moments right before the world found out! Before Prince's face would be plastered all over CNN, and MSNBC, and every other major news network. Before "1999", "Little Red Corvette", and countless other hits would blast from TV screens, and speakers, on an incessant loop.

Those were the moments when only a few people outside the walls of Prince's purple paradise were beginning to understand what had happened behind closed doors—that Prince, one of the greatest artists of all time, was dead.

In that moment, though, with Rodney on one line and John on the other, I didn't believe it. I didn't want to believe it.

"You want me to know what, Rodney? I don't know what you're talking about."

"Oh, Kim." His voice was barely above a whisper. "You haven't heard about Prince?"

I tried to shake off his ominous tone. "I saw an article on TMZ about something going down at Paisley, but that's a gossip magazine! They claim people are dead all the time, so—"

"Kim." he interrupted. "The coroner just pulled off. And Prince, is in, the van."

His words were sharp and pointed, immediately piercing the soft of my heart.

My mind went vacant and my own horrifying screams filled the car all around me. I couldn't move. I couldn't think. I could barely breathe. For four-and-a-half hours I sat in a barbershop parking lot, unmoving, and in utter shock.

Just like that, I had lost my longest and best client. I lost a friend, a confidante. More importantly, I lost my brother.

"A Promise 2 see Jesus in the morning light"[3]

—From the song "Thunder" by Prince

But I should rewind a little bit. Because even though you and I may have been shocked by Prince's death, I can confirm that Prince was fully prepared for his fate.

On April 1, 2016, twenty days before he died, Prince told me that the end was near. Call it a spiritual connection with God, or just an innate intuition, but he knew it! He *felt* it. And with the same conviction that he'd used to predict the deaths of Michael Jackson, Whitney Houston, and even Anna Nicole Smith, he foreshadowed the end of his own life.

That prophecy may have given him some sense of calm, or understanding, about what lay ahead. But for me, there was no peace to be had. I had spent nearly 30 years with Prince and had traveled the world with him on one adventure after another. He was my brother! I was his sister. And, when I received that news, my heart shattered for the loss of my family.

As I sat in the barbershop parking lot, I'm sure people walking by my car thought I was losing my mind. I was, in a way. I alternated between silent sobs and fits of rage.

Eventually, Rodney went live at CBS, the TMZ article

got even more clicks, and the rest of the world learned what I was still struggling to comprehend. I realized this as my phone started blowing up, starting with my best friend, Cosetta. She called back to back, only getting out a few words each time before I hung up, preferring the silence and solitude of my car over her well-meaning but insufficient "thoughts and prayers." Cosetta wanted to know where I was and whether she could come get me. But I refused.

I got so many calls from friends and family members, as well as every other celebrity hairstylist I knew, that my phone literally shut itself off! They wanted to know if the reports were true! How I was holding up. And, when I was too weak to respond, my iPhone did the work for me, shutting out the world to leave me alone in my grief. I felt lost and confused, and every time I'd think I was okay and pull myself back together, the tears and screams would kick in again, reminding me that it wasn't okay at all.

I sat there for hours, delirious, until I finally had enough composure to get out of the car. It wasn't until I went inside and saw Woods, a barber I've known for years that I realized I'd pulled up in front of his shop. I was too hysterical to notice before.

Woods looked surprised to see me—even more so when I told him how long I'd been sitting outside. I wasn't sure I could drive myself home.

"We heard about Prince," he said, eyes on the floor. "I wasn't sure it was real since I hadn't heard anything from you."

I looked up at the flat screen TV on the wall and caught a glimpse of Prince, clad in a deep plum suit and a gold, silk shirt, dancing with Beyonce at the 2004 Grammys. I felt my knees buckle. "It's definitely real."

"Okay," Woods said, rushing to my side and grabbing my right elbow. "I'm gonna take you home."

He walked me outside, opened the passenger door of my car, and helped me in. He must have put the key in the ignition at some point, started the car, and drove off, but I don't remember. I was in a daze, only starting to piece together the totality of my loss, of the world's loss. Looking back, I don't even remember Woods pulling up to my house, or me walking from my car to the front door. I do not recall unlocking the front door, or walking to my bedroom and collapsing on the floor, either.

But I do remember calling Gina Rivera, founder of Phenix Salon Suites, where I still teach hair coloring classes. (She was a featured entrepreneur on CBS's *Undercover Boss*.)

"He's dead," I said, without introduction.

Gina sighed heavily. "I know. I've been waiting to hear from you. You okay?"

I didn't respond.

"Well at least tell me what you need," she said. "How can I help you?"

I looked around the room, and my eyes landed on the suitcase lying open on the floor, spilling over with jeans, some shirts, and a pair of boots. My bag was never fully unpacked because I never knew when Prince would call and tell me that a car was picking me up in an hour to catch a redeye flight to Paris, Toronto, or Egypt. I needed to be ready at all times, and in that moment, I was grateful for the training. I rushed over and started pushing the clothes back into the suitcase.

"I need plane tickets and a hotel room," I said. "I need to get to Paisley."

Gina didn't hesitate. "You got it."

Within minutes, my daughter Sieara and I were headed to the airport; hours later we were in the air.

On the flight, I thought about the day I officially met Prince, the day when, instead of stopping by my salon to get his hair done, he called and told me that a driver was on his way, that I needed to get to LAX immediately.

That night, nearly three decades before, had been the first time I'd set foot outside of California. To be honest, it was the first time I'd left Inglewood, and when I landed in Minneapolis, as I saw snow for the first time. I struggled to pull my flimsy jacket tight around my chest; I could barely contain my excitement. I couldn't begin to imagine all the adventures that I would take with the creative genius known as Prince Rogers Nelson!

But there was no excitement when I arrived in Minnesota on April 21, 2016, only dread. I knew that once I got to Paisley I would come face-to-face with the reality of Prince's death and of what happened to him, and that frightened me. I was also nervous about seeing his body, even though I knew I would have to. I needed to see him to know that it was real, that he was gone and not coming back. And I needed to see him to prepare him for the funeral. There was no way anyone else was going to put their hands on his head—or slay his mane one last time—but me.

Sieara and I checked into our hotel, and I immediately called Kirk, Prince's bodyguard, to tell him that I was in town and on my way to Paisley to see Prince. When I heard him say "no," that I couldn't see Prince, I jerked the phone away from my ear and stared at it in disbelief.

"This is not a game!" I said, frantically. "Where is he? I need to say goodbye!"

There was silence from Kirk and then, finally, a whisper. "I'm sorry, Kim, but it's too late. He's already gone."

"What do you mean, 'too late'?" I asked, my voice catching.

"I'm so sorry," he said again, "but it didn't have anything to do with me."

All at once, the truth that I would never see Prince again suffocated me. "But why wouldn't you at least let me see him?" I pleaded. *"Why can't I see him?"*

My begging made no difference, though. Kirk was right. It was out of his hands.

"It" was a reference to Prince's cremation, a process that was already complete, per the instructions of Prince's sister, Tyka Nelson. She

"It's ok to fear the answers, but you can't avoid them. They are training ground for the process."[4]

—From the movie, *A Wrinkle in Time*

had been allowed to sit with his body for two hours beforehand. The rest of us—the band, and other employees who got in the trenches with him daily, as well as those, like me, who were closest to him, whom he so affectionately called family—could not say our farewells.

If I hadn't already been drifting through a heavy fog, barely managing to put one foot in front of the other, I would have surely broken down. But I was already broken.

I was also aware that something wasn't right. Burning Prince's body within hours of his death didn't make any good sense, let alone bad sense. And unlike the rest of the world, I knew the in's and out's of the fraught relationship he had with his sister and the rest of his biological family.

While Prince had always made sure that Tyka's financial

needs were met, he had chosen to love her from afar. She had her (well-documented) issues with drugs, and he was careful to ensure that those issues didn't infiltrate his life. I was there when things started to change, however, when the gates started to lift, and the tightknit crew that he had cultivated for so long started to fray at the edges. I saw him let people into his life that hadn't been there for over two decades. So, in retrospect, I probably shouldn't have been surprised by how his death was handled.

But I was! And it hurt like hell.

I called my mother, who had been my rock throughout my entire journey with Prince, keeping me strong and praying me over each mountaintop and through each muck-filled valley. With tears strangling my words, I told her that I had gotten to Minneapolis too late. That Prince had already been taken away, my chance to say goodbye stolen. She prayed for me like she always had, this time reminding me that while I didn't get those final minutes alone with him that I wanted, I had nearly 30 years of memories to carry me through my pain.

I hung up and stretched across my hotel bed, still fully dressed. My mother was right! But that didn't soothe my brokenness, or make the agony any easier to bear. My daughter, Sieara, held my hand in silence, our shared misery overwhelming the small room. I was drowning in my own thoughts, wondering if we could have done anything differently—if *I* could have done anything differently. Meanwhile, Prince's image and music were being broadcast on every TV channel, a constant reminder of what I had with Prince, and what I now had lost.

My last call was with Sheila E's personal assistant, who told me that Prince's memorial service would be at Paisley the next morning. Sheila wanted me there, and I wanted to be there, but after the cremation drama, I had my concerns.

"Will they let me in?" I asked. "Nobody's gonna be tripping, are they?"

"Look," she said, her voice taut, "you just need to get here as early as you can. Whoever gets here is who's going to get in, so just get here."

I tossed the phone onto the nightstand and stared at the ceiling until my eyelids were too heavy to stay open.

If I wanted to write the day after Prince's death as a movie script, I would leave the weather exactly as it was—cold, wet, and dreary.

"Blow that devil away. Eye No . . ." [5]

—From the song "Eye No" by Prince

The morning of the memorial, I dressed quickly in jeans and a long-sleeved t-shirt. Aside from my need to get to Paisley as soon as possible, I had no desire to impress anybody. Over my clothes I put on the first real winter coat I purchased after I started traveling with Prince. My California blood was no match for the harsh, northern winters, and after a few days of chattering teeth, and a nonstop runny nose, I picked up the first thing that could protect me from the wind and snow. As I pulled the coat's zipper up to my throat, that memory sent the first tears of the day cascading down my cheeks.

By the time I arrived at Paisley Park, there were hundreds of thousands of people standing at the gates. It was mayhem, with some people wailing in distress, their faces red from the frigid temperatures and their crying. Others broke out into choruses of their favorite Prince songs, and all around were at least a dozen police officers determined to make sure nothing too crazy happened. The guards at the Paisley gates were on point, securing the entrance like their very lives depended on it. They were so determined to keep out any fans that they were mistakenly blocking long-time Prince employees from entering. Thankfully, Sheila E popped her head outside and told them to let me in.

Inside the Paisley walls, the air was thick and somber. I had been inside the compound too many times to count, sometimes living there for months at a time, but it had never felt like this before. The joy and creativity that used to greet everyone at the door were buried under heartache and echoes of softly playing music. Staffers walked solemnly around a purple urn sitting in the middle of the atrium floor, sometimes stopping to whisper soft words in Prince's memory, but I chose to stand silently in the back.

I believe that memorials should be festive affairs, where folks gather for a cheerful celebration of life. This wasn't that. It was bad enough that there wasn't a formal event planned to honor Prince, and no way to bring closure to friends and fans. But even this opportunity for those closest to him to pay final respects was more gloomy than glorious.

Back on the outside, though, the atmosphere was electric! Everyone was emotional, and no one was shy about showing it. Eventually, I left the atrium and made my way back to the other side of the gates, preferring to remember Prince alongside those who had gathered in freezing temperatures to say goodbye with those who had never been closer to him than they were that dreary morning.

I hadn't been outside long when a black SUV pulled up to the curb. As soon as the vehicle came to a stop, the back door swung open, and Mayte Garcia, Prince's first wife, jumped out. She ran over to me. Her eyeliner was smudged and cheeks flushed. We hugged and cried. She was a wreck! Wondering why Prince had to leave us when he did, and what she could have done to prevent it. In response, I told her what I was only beginning to accept: that there was nothing anyone could have done to change his fate. Prince was a man of his own means and in full control of his life, so if none of us were there the day he took his last breath that was how God had intended it to be. I held Mayte even tighter and told her just that. I told her that everything happens for a reason, and I tried to bring her peace even as I wrestled with my own emotions.

I realized that people had been watching the interaction between Mayte, and myself, whom they all recognized as Prince's ex. So, once she got back in her SUV to leave, they began whispering and pointing, asking if anyone knew who I was, and what role I'd played in Prince's life. Donna Gregory, Mayte's former makeup artist, was standing outside in the crowd, and when she heard the questions she jumped right in, introducing me to the fans, and news crews, as Prince's long-time hairstylist. I smiled and gave myself a quick pep talk, forcing myself to be a pillar of support for those who were devastated by Prince's death despite never having had a single conversation with him. Just like that, I was thrown in front of cameras to talk about my brother's life, our relationship, and unfortunately, his passing.

Despite battling with my own questions and lack of answers, I talked to as many people as I could, answering their questions and trying to soothe their broken hearts with my personal memories. I understood that with Prince gone hearing my stories was the closest they'd ever come to hearing from the man himself.

All along the fence around Paisley, fans that had traveled hundreds of miles had honored Prince, placing bags of nacho cheese-flavored Doritos and pancake mix (two of his favorite foods) next to purple balloons and handwritten notes. Donna, Sieara, and I walked this path along with Jon, who had been a driver in Prince's camp. We passed flowers, and cards, and stuffed animals—all the gifts of love that piled up for four or five months before anyone collected them, clearing away the personal offerings from fans who had journeyed from all corners of the world to pay final respects.

I went back to my hotel that evening feeling drained, but I took comfort in the fact that I was comforting others. And the next morning, when we learned that the fans were still there, still standing at the Paisley gates, I decided to join them. I went back to the gates for two more days, still answering questions, still willing to share the pieces of Prince that I kept with me with all who would come. On our last day, Sieara knelt down and signed a banner that some fans had stretched along the fence. It was a written farewell, and thousands of people had already added their names. For Sieara, it was also a moving tribute to the man she called Uncle P, the man she considered a friend and loved like family.

When I finally left Paisley for good, and boarded my flight to L.A., I wasn't any closer to coming to terms with Prince's death, mainly because I still had so many questions that hadn't been answered. I was grieving, yes, but I was also baffled and angry. Despite the rainbow that shone in the sky the day after he died, the air had been icy, with snow blanketing the ground. As so many people pointed out, the weather was a perfect manifestation of Prince's song, "Sometimes it Snows in April." It also perfectly matched my mood.

Back home in California, I sunk into a dark place. For months, I worked and went through the day-to-day motions of life, but things never really returned to normal. At the forefront of my mind was the constant reminder that I would never get another call from him, that we would never watch another movie together or share another laugh. Then I received an email from a fan that changed everything.

> *"I alone cannot change the world, but I can carry a stone across the water to create many ripples."*[6]
>
> —**Mother Teresa**

Can you believe it's been six months since he passed?

I stared at the small black words on the screen and blinked away tears. *6 months?* I couldn't believe it at all. So much time had elapsed, but I hadn't noticed because I was just stumbling and fumbling through life, too numb to live fully!

I was still in pain, still missing him dearly, but I also felt that I needed to get up and do something. I thought about how I'd felt when I talked to the fans after Prince's death—how much of a blessing it had been for me to share with them, and how grateful they'd been for me to take the time to do so. It was then, reading that email, when the fog finally lifted. I knew I had to come forward to tell my story—to tell *our* story.

It's the same whenever any influential music artist passes. Once the last tribute concert has aired, and the posthumous record has been released, someone—a former manager or spouse, or a childhood best friend—writes a book. It's marketed as the real, behind-the-scenes, never-been-told story, the one that none of us could ever know from simply watching music videos and memorizing song lyrics.

Well, Prince was larger than life, and one of the greatest artists this world has ever seen. So, it's no wonder that, in the two short years since his passing, we've already seen the publication of multiple books. On top of that, there's been little attention paid to how well the authors actually knew Prince. But I get it. To be in Prince's presence was to understand that you were a part of living history. Now that he's gone, people want to share their small piece of history with the world.

Whether it's the women Prince loved or the women who loved him; the band members and stage crew who ensured his shows were perfect night after night; his "chosen" family members, who were closer than blood, but so distant in every other way; or the litany of assistants, attorneys, and other staffers who managed the day-to-day affairs so that Prince could focus on his music—there are many people with a story to tell.

On the surface, I am just one of those people. Yet upon closer look, it is clear that what I have to share is entirely different.

Being Prince's hairstylist for nearly 29 years, as Pops used to say, I kept him "fried, dyed, and laid to the side!" Helping him regularly reinvent himself was a must, and I experimented with a slew of products to keep his hair soft, and healthy, as a part of his daily beauty regimen. In maintaining his sexy, we kept those sandy brown roots a fabulous blue-black hue, so that his outer appearance always matched his youthful, inner energy. But my relationship with Prince was so much more than that.

As anyone with hair will tell you, the relationship between a client and trusted hairstylist is worth much more than some laid edges and tamed roots! The stylist becomes a confidant and counselor, her chair like a comfy couch in a therapist's office! This is the relationship I had with Prince. Over the course of nearly three decades, he shared everything with me, from his professional highs to his personal lows. I was there for countless award ceremonies and hall of fame inductions. I shared in his joy when he stood up against the music industry... *and won*! I was there for not one, but two, failed marriages, as well as the tragic death of his two children. I witnessed the strained relationships with his relatives while providing a nonjudgmental ear when he described the hurts of his childhood.

Prince was always surrounded by music, and musicians; whether they were his newest protégées, or icons in their own right. They all just wanted to hang out and jam! But our connection ran deeper than the music. I knew the *man*, and I believe my assignment in his life was pre-ordained by God. I occupied the space between his life and his art. And my distance from the music provided the foundation for our decades-long friendship.

Prince and I had a spiritual connection away from the sold-out arenas and the cheering crowds, the sexy lyrics, and the funky bass lines. Whether he was stripping away his latest band to embark on his acoustic Piano and a Microphone tour, or filing for a divorce, our friendship stood strong. To put it simply, Prince trusted me. He trusted me with his hair, and more importantly, he trusted me with his heart. That's a trust that I refused to violate when he was alive, so I definitely won't violate it in his death.

I will share stories—of the time we explored the pyramids in Egypt; walked among the snow glaciers in Switzerland, and visited the ICE HOTEL, the world's first hotel made entirely of ice and snow; and when we stayed in a haunted castle, and rode horseback along the Continental Divide in Colorado. But this book isn't a tell-all, or a salacious airing of dirty laundry. It is instead, an effort to shed light on Prince as a man. A spiritual being, clothed in flesh, just as if God was one of us.

For fans who are still reeling from his death, and who feel robbed of closure, this book will detail parts of his life that he never shared, including the intense joy, and crushing agony he felt, after laying eyes on his son for the first time—and then having to make the decision to take him off life support. In reading, you will understand the responsibility that he felt to share his gift with you, and how that obligation kept him in the studio, creating, for days at a time. You will also understand the gratification he felt when helping some of his biggest musical influences take back control of their own music careers.

In these pages, I will also share my journey—from South Central L.A., to Minneapolis, and around the world more times than I could have ever dreamed! I want you to know how I mustered the courage to walk up to Prince, a complete unknown, to show him my portfolio and market my services. And, I want you to understand that if you are willing to take risks, and step out on faith, God will do more than you could ever think, hope, or imagine, for you too!

Nearly three years after his death, and with fans around the world still clamoring for more of his life, there are more books that will be written, even after this one. But this book is different. This one comes from someone who walked with Prince for nearly 29 years. Who grew up with him, and saw him through the best and worst of life.

This book, you can trust, is the truth.

CUT

The Cut of a diamond is its only quality completely shaped by external factors. Various instruments carve and slice, revealing shape, style, and symmetry, as well as the lines and angles that determine how well the diamond reflects and disperses light. When finished, it is the Cut that determines the brilliance of the diamond and, ultimately, its beauty.

One of the first things people ask me after finding out that I worked with Prince for nearly 29 years is, "How did you meet him?"

It's a funny story, actually, and it starts in a McDonald's!

I went to high school, in the Valley, in the 1980s. There were only a handful of black students there, at the time. Naturally, we looked out for each other. Sharing class notes, or passing word about which teachers to avoid, and which students weren't too thrilled about our presence. I've always been the nurturing type, and I especially kept my eye out for the black students who were younger than me. Curtis, Ronu, and Marlon were three guys that I took under my wing from the beginning of their high school careers. They were only a year younger than me, but they were so small in stature that I couldn't help but treat them like my little brothers. I'd stop them in the hallway to see if they'd finished their homework and make sure they weren't getting into any trouble, or I'd smooth things over with an upperclassman if they got caught up in some mess! Often, they repaid the sentiment by serenading me… with a rap song.

L.A. Dream Team, a local rap group, dropped their song "Rockberry Jam" in 1985. Their success kicked off the west coast hip-hop scene. Paving the way for artists like World Class Wreckin' Cru and NWA, and we couldn't get enough of their first big hit! We played the song at parties, blasted it from car stereos, and jammed to it with our Walkmans! And because of the song's title and infectious hook—"Ahhh, Rockberry! Rockberry!"—Curtis, Ronu, and Marlon decided it should be my theme song.

It didn't matter whether I was walking to class or grabbing lunch in the cafeteria, if the boys saw me, they started rapping immediately: "Ahhh, Kim Berry! Kim Berry!" Then one of them would start banging his hands on a wall or table to simulate drums, while another would beatbox to fill in the rest of the beat. They gathered a small crowd with their first few shows, but eventually, the other students of El Camino Real High School got used to the impromptu concerts and went on about their business, not giving the "El Camino Dream Team" a second thought. I got used to it, too, until I realized the "Kim Berry Jam" would follow me outside of school!

It was mid-summer, and I had just picked up some fresh K-Swiss' at the Slauson Swap Meet. I walked into the nearby McDonald's, ready to order some nuggets and fries, but before I could get to the counter, those fools started beating on the table and rapping!

"Ahhh, Kim Berry! Kim Berry!"

Slightly embarrassed to be serenaded away from school, I was searching the room to see where Curtis, Ronu, and Marlon were sitting, when my eyes landed on a table in the middle of the restaurant. There were five or six guys huddled around a taller, dark-skinned dude, leaning in and hanging on his every word like he was the messiah and they were his disciples. I recognized the leader as the lifeguard from our neighborhood pool. I also knew he did some DJ-ing for a local company that traveled around the country throwing big parties for teenagers. They were called Uncle Jamm's Army, and they were celebrity DJs, before celebrity DJs were actually a thing!

As I waited on my food, I continued to peep him out of the corner of my eye. He looked pompous and arrogant, dressed in head-to-toe FILA, with gazelle glasses, and perfect finger waves. It took me all of two seconds to guess that he had more girls than a Too Short video.

Nuggets in hand, I was heading for the door when his friends, Duke and David, jumped in front of me. "Hey! Kim Berry!"

I spun around and met the dudes eye-to-eye. "Excuse me?" I said. "Do I know you?" I was about to ask how they knew my name, but before the words could get out of my mouth, I remembered: "Ahhh, Kim Berry! Kim Berry!"

I shook my head and laughed.

"Hey, my homeboy Coco wants to talk to you," the friend said, motioning over to his leader still commanding court at the middle table.

I crossed my arms and let my McDonald's bag dangle from my right hand. "What's the matter with him? He can't talk?"

"He doesn't need to talk. Just put your number down on the paper so he can holla at you. I'm telling you, he's feeling you."

I looked over at the table again. It didn't look like Coco was feeling anything other than himself, or maybe the burger he was munching on, but I gave his friend my number anyway. I didn't give him much thought as I went back home and worked on an essay that was due the next day. To my surprise, Coco called that night.

Coco reminded me of my dad in a lot of ways. If Coco

wasn't at the pool or DJ-ing, he was selling mixtapes out of his car, trying to earn some extra cash. Likewise, my dad was a hustler through and through, and he did whatever he needed to in order to take care of his family. If the cabinets were bare, and I woke up and said I wanted Cap'n Crunch for breakfast, my dad would crawl out of bed, get in his car, and not come back until he had my box of cereal. Not only did my dad keep a 9-5 as a supervisor, with the Granatelli Company, overseeing the manufacture of supercharged motorsport engines. He also ran the neighborhood bookie joint, had an early-morning paper route (that my brothers and I often worked), and owned a hamburger stand. One of my dad's favorite lines was, "If I got $100 in my pocket, I'm broke." In short, he kept money flowing and kept me happy, and Coco was no different.

My relationship with Coco progressed pretty quickly. He was my first boyfriend, first love, first *everything*. And even though all the girls wanted him, he took pride in being with me and taking care of me. We did the usual things that young couples do: shopping at the mall, going to dinner and to the movies, hanging with friends, and listening to music. And like a lot of teens, I snuck out of the house to be with him, telling my parents that I was hanging out with my girlfriends and praying that nothing would ever go wrong. Many times, we hung out at industry events, where Coco would introduce me to his DJ and musician friends.

Being with Coco was my first real view of the entertainment industry. It was a true behind-the-scenes look at how one man could engage and entertain thousands. He had made a name for himself spinning records, and the more people he knew, the more opportunities seemed to just flow his way. Within a couple years of us getting together, Coco had gone from DJ-ing parties with other local celebrities, including rapper/producer/ DJ Egyptian Lover, to working as a bodyguard. His clients included the R&B group Shai, as well as hometown rappers Candyman, Ice Cube, and Mack 10. Soon enough, he landed the client that would change his life, and mine, forever.

Quite frankly, I shouldn't have been with Coco at all. He was three years older than me and already out of school, and I know my daddy would have killed me if he knew how serious we were. But there was an undeniable appeal of being with a man who was cute and charismatic, who everybody knew, and wanted to be close to, who was happy to share his every success with me.

Those were the best of times, but I never wanted to rely on Coco completely. I made sure to have my own thing going on, and even though I thought I was just biding my time, I had no idea what the universe had in mind.

"4 U Eye shall B wild"[7]

—From the song "Anna Stesia" by Prince

I never dreamed of being a celebrity hairstylist, or even a hairstylist at all, when I was growing up. My plan was to study medicine and become a doctor. I stayed out of trouble and hit the books hard, so much so, that I graduated high school at 16. I was proud of myself, but also tired. So, I decided to take a year off before going to college. They call it a "gap year" now, but back then, I just knew that I had busted my butt to get through school without any issues, and I needed to chill for a minute.

We lived in the hood, where trouble lurked around every corner. Whether your vice was drugs, sex, gang banging, or just being in the streets, access was easy and constant. Because I knew I was under intense scrutiny as the youngest kid, and the only girl in my family, I made it a point to be a good kid.

Honestly, even if my parents had let me run free, I still wouldn't have acted a fool. My father was my world; he was my king; he was a superhero in my eyes. And there was no way I was going to disappoint my father.

My parents kept me involved in a constant flow of cheerleading, drill team, and pep club (of which I was the president). For whatever sports the boys was doing, I was on the sidelines cheering. This continual activity served two purposes: In addition to making it impossible to run the streets, staying busy helped me to learn the value of hard work very early in my life. I watched my dad hold down his job as well as multiple side hustles, while my mom worked her full-time gig and maintained a household. Needless to say, I didn't think twice about long afternoons of cheerleading or pep club practice after school, followed by even more hours of homework. I did what my parents told me, when they told me to do it, and since I'd worked hard, maintained good grades, gotten my diploma, and hadn't gotten pregnant like a lot of other girls in the hood, I felt like I'd earned the right to take a break.

On top of that, I was also feeling really discouraged about my future career plans. My heart was still set on becoming a doctor, but a conversation with my high school counselor made me second-guess whether it was actually possible. Despite graduating in the top 10% of my class, the counselor told me that I didn't have the qualifications to go to a four-year school and that I should, instead, think about junior college. I was devastated and confused! I was intelligent and had never had an issue keeping up with my classes, so I didn't know what more I could have done to prove myself to be college-bound.

As it turned out, the counselor's concern wasn't my academic record—it was the color of my skin. Many years later, we learned that she gave the same junior college advice to every one of the black students who walked into her office. (Some of the former students who knew they were more than qualified to pursue their bachelor's degree ended up filing a class-action lawsuit against the counselor. I didn't participate in the suit, but things still turned out pretty well for me when I enrolled in the University of Prince Rogers Nelson.)

I didn't know about the counselor's ulterior motives at the time. I could only listen to her advice, as instructed by school administrators, and try to work through my emotions on my own.

Now, to be clear, my mom didn't care about my discouragement, or my exhaustion. She had initially agreed to my year off, but after a couple of months of side-eyeing me as I spent my days watching TV, or lounging on the coach, she shut that down real quick! "Either you go to school or get a job, or you gotta get up out my house!" she said, throwing her hand on her hip and twisting her mouth into a don't-play-with-me scowl. "There's only one queen in this castle, and that's me."

I shouldn't have been surprised, honestly. Even though my dad worked overtime to provide for us, my mom worked, too. She was a kept woman who still kept a job just because she felt like it. And she kept all of her own money, too. My dad covered the household bills, and my mom used her money for anything extra. She would take my brothers and me (and sometimes all the neighborhood kids) to Magic Mountain or Disneyland. Or, she'd spend her nights playing B.I.N.G.O. My mom's favorite thing to do, though, was throw a party. We had rent parties, birthday parties, pokeno and tonk parties, and all sorts of other get-togethers that would justify the need to invite every single person in a 15-mile radius! There was always more than enough drinks, food, and music to go around. And, we didn't have to worry about disturbing the neighbors because, more than likely, they were around back with a cup of kool-aid in one hand and a plate of ribs in the other.

My mom was the grande dame of every single event at our house, and even when she wasn't throwing a party, she still ruled the roost. Needless to say, she wasn't about to have me sitting around the house doing nothing.

The day my mom confronted me, I stormed right out the front door and walked down the street to Pacific Beauty College. She hadn't suggested that I go to hair school, and it certainly hadn't been on my mind before that day. She just told me to get up and go do something, and the beauty school was the first "something" that crossed my path.

When I walked in the door I ran right into Mr. Goines, the owner of the school. He was a short, brown-skinned man with glasses and a jheri curl, and he was passionate about hair.

"I'm only here because I need something to do before I go to college next year," I explained. I didn't want him to be confused about my intentions, or to think that I was trying to make a career of this.

"Great!" Mr. Goines said, "This is just a one-year program. Twelve months from now you'll be one of the finest hairstylists in L.A."

I sucked my teeth and crossed my arms but managed to reply with a simple "Okay." I didn't want Mr. Goines to think I was too excited about doing hair, because I wasn't, but I didn't have a plan B, either! If I didn't find a productive way to fill up my days before college, my ass was gonna be out on the street.

After our conversation Mr. Goines walked me around the building, telling me how everything worked and what to expect. He pointed out the shampoo and styling areas and showed me the floor where I would get to work with actual clients. Mr. Goines assured me that I'd do well, even though I had no idea how to style hair and wasn't sure I could actually learn in one year. But his confidence was infectious, and before I knew it, I was signing on the dotted enrollment line.

I went back home and threw the paperwork on the table in front of my mom. "I hope you're happy," I said.

She didn't even look up from the book she was reading. "Hmph. I hope *you're* happy."

My mother couldn't have cared less about me going to beauty school. She just wanted me off the couch and making better use of my time. I didn't care about beauty school either; I just needed to keep her off my back. But neither of us knew that she had actually pushed me right into my destiny, and that push couldn't have been more perfectly timed. Shortly after I started at Pacific, Coco got the job of a lifetime when he became Prince's bodyguard.

The world—to say the least of the actual music industry—wasn't ready for Prince Rogers Nelson.

The story goes that when executives at Warner Brothers first heard Prince's demo, they thought it was a full band of five or six musicians laying the track. The idea that it could be one crazy-talented multi-instrumentalist on the tape was just inconceivable. Even Jimmy Jam, the super-producer behind multi-platinum smashes including Boyz II Men's "On Bended Knee," Usher's "U Remind Me," and a slew of Janet Jackson records, admitted to being intimidated by Prince's musicianship when they met as junior high classmates.

But being able to jump from keys, to drums, to bass, and, of course, guitar wasn't the only marker of Prince's otherworldly genius. He was also one of the greatest songwriters, performers, and singers who ever lived. These were all gifts that had manifested in Prince when he was a child, going all the way back to the time he taught himself to play the "Batman" theme song on piano. Along the way, he enjoyed working with other talented people, whether they were his classmates, like Jimmy Jam, or family members.

Tyka, Prince's sister, also had a gift for singing and was one of the first artists he worked to develop. He wrote songs for her, and in addition to helping her find her voice; he also tried to help her land a record deal. I don't know if Warner Brothers was the first, or only, label that took an interest in Tyka, but I know that they did—and that the meeting with Warner Brothers kicked off a decades-long rift between the two siblings. Years later, Prince told me that when Warner Brothers execs passed on Tyka it added fuel to their long-burning discord and was just enough to sever the relationship completely. Even worse, Prince walked out with a deal for himself.

Truthfully, Prince had been waiting on his breakthrough for years. Once he found his gift and realized that he had been created to make music, there was no turning back. Music wasn't just something he was passionate about; it was also the very thing that would deliver him from a childhood of trauma. Prince's parents divorced when he was still young, and as a result, he was a victim of poverty and many of the other abuses that often arise when couples split. Those early injustices have a way of sticking with a person, and I will never forget the day Prince let me know just how much his childhood experiences still impacted his life as an adult.

Prince was always excited to see my daughter, Sieara, when I brought her around. Far from the standoffish celebrity people may have thought he was, Prince could open up and relate to anyone, especially kids. He was close with all of the staff's children, who each referred to Prince as Uncle P, and weren't at all concerned about how many number-one records he had. Uncle P was a friend who they could talk to, and laugh with, and who treated them with honor and respect.

On one occasion, Sieara and I were sitting in the living

room of a suite at the Beverly Hills Hotel, catching up with Prince while I did his hair. Sieara had been filling Prince in about everything that was happening at school and with her friends, and then started telling him a story—one that started with "Mom," ended with "took money out of my piggy bank," and left out all of the important details in between. Never mind the lack of supporting facts. When Prince heard that I had taken Sieara's money, he jumped out of my chair so fast I almost singed the back of his neck with my flat iron.

"What do you mean, she took money from your piggy bank?" he asked my daughter, with anger creasing his forehead. Sieara and I had been laughing, thinking this silly misunderstanding wasn't that big of a deal. But we saw quickly that Prince thought otherwise.

I started to explain the details of the story that Sieara had omitted, telling him that I needed to wash clothes at the laundromat and took $10 worth of quarters out of her piggy bank. I also told him that I replaced her coins with a $10 bill, but it didn't matter. Prince was having none of it.

"Don't you *ever* take money from that child, do you hear me!?" he spat, finally facing me. "You have no idea what that will do to her as she grows up."

I stood in slack-jawed silence while I finished his hair, unsure how I should respond, or whether I should respond at all. It was obvious that Sieara's revelation had had an emotional impact on him, and later, when she took a nap, he explained why. Prince told me that his mother had been addicted to drugs, and once, when she ran out of cash and couldn't get money from his stepfather. She snuck into Prince's room and took what she could find. He had been saving that money for a new guitar.

For the rest of his life, that moment clung to Prince like the smell of grease from a fish fry. It impacted the way he trusted and treated women; it forced him to protect his music—and his money—fiercely; and, of course, it made clear the reality that in order for him to achieve success and stability, he was going to have work tirelessly and do it on his own, proving every naysayer wrong.

By the time *Purple Rain* took over airwaves and movie screens in the mid-80s, there was no doubt that Prince was the funky musical savant we never knew we were looking for! Once Coco became Prince's bodyguard, I was willing to do whatever it took to land my own spot in his camp. The only problem was that my relationship with Coco was built on him taking care of me. There was no way he was going to refer me for a job that paid more than he was making.

But all hope wasn't lost. After about a year of Coco saying, "Nah, it ain't the right time," over and over again when I asked to be introduced, God allowed me another way in.

Coco may not have wanted to help me get a job with Prince, but he still invited me to hang out on set during his video or photo shoots. Each time, I'd hang out with Coco a little bit, waiting until just the right moment to break away and find the folks in charge of Prince's glam: the clothes, the hair, the makeup. Prince's style was as innovative and undeniable as his music, and I wanted to meet the people who were making it all happen.

Prince's hairstylist was Tanya, a twenty-something sista with a smart mouth. We hit it off immediately! It didn't take long for her to start reaching out to me directly (instead of through Coco) whenever she came to L.A. Sometimes I'd stop by her hotel to hang out, or we'd meet at a club. No matter what we did, though, the conversation was easy, and our friendship developed organically, like we were just regular home girls from around the way. All the while I was careful not to ask for favors, or to invite myself to different events with her. I didn't want to come off as thirsty, or needy. Nor did I want Tanya to think I was a star-trapper trying to get close to her so I could get close to Prince.

Still, I knew there was a lot that I could learn from Tanya. She was a successful celebrity stylist, and I was fresh out of beauty school. I hadn't ever considered working for an entertainer, but Tanya showed me that it was possible, and with my daddy's hustler spirit coursing through my veins, I figured, why not?

I started paying close attention to how Tanya set up her table before she styled Prince, and then I went out and duplicated her table. When she picked up a new gel or moisturizer, I went and got that, too. In the meantime, I also pressed clothes, ran errands, fetched coffee, and did whatever I needed to do in order to look like I had a reason for being there. This was important because Prince was noticing me. He didn't say anything, ever, but I knew he was watching. Always. He would come backstage, say something to Tanya, look at me, and walk back out, flipping the occasional side eye over his shoulder as he sauntered away. It wasn't until later, when I had become Prince's hairstylist, that I understood how difficult it was for him to trust people and how he was always aware when there was someone new hanging around.

At that time, I ignored his sideways glances. My plan was simply to be ready, so that when the right opportunity arose, I wouldn't have to *get* ready. I just had no idea how soon that opportunity would come.

"Girl, I think I'm gonna quit," Tanya said one day, all casual, like she wasn't spilling a Boston's party worth of tea.

Tanya and I were sitting around at a photo shoot, waiting on Prince to arrive. We had been talking and hanging out like normal, but I could tell that something was bothering her. She seemed frustrated and angry, like whatever mess she had been holding onto was about to bust right out of her. Even still, I wasn't expecting her to say that she was going to quit a job I would kill for.

"Are you crazy?!" I said. "Prince is one of the biggest artists, and *you have the best job in the world.* Why would you quit?"

Tanya rolled her eyes. "You don't even know the half. Everything ain't always what it seems."

I was waiting on her to say something else, maybe to explain what could be so bad about working for a musical legend, but the conversation was already over. Tanya walked back over to her station and started packing her stuff. She never said anything else about it, and neither did I. But she didn't have to. My mother taught me that words are powerful—when you speak them out of your mouth, they have a high likelihood of coming true. Sure enough, it wasn't too long after Tanya first told me her plan that she and Prince got into an argument on set. It was such a little thing that I don't even remember what the argument was about, but it was the perfect time for those words she spoke to manifest.

> *"Don't wait for opportunities to come to you, create your own."*[8]
>
> —Mr. Berry (Pops)

"My lips are chapped from kissing your little black ass!" she shouted on her way out the door. And just like that, Prince was without a hairstylist.

I didn't immediately set out to get Tanya's job, but I knew that if I had the chance to prove myself, I would definitely be ready. Even though I was clueless about what I was actually preparing for, I had spent nine months training for the opportunity that was set before me. Finally, a few months after Tanya walked out, on Christmas Eve, 1988, I had the chance to put my preparation to the test.

I was sitting at home alone when Coco called and told me that Prince would be at a club in West Hollywood. I was so excited I didn't have time to say thank you before slamming the phone down and rushing to change clothes. Always in the mind of staying ready, my portfolio was stacked with models, even though I wasn't sure if, or when, I'd ever need it. After I threw on a dress, I looked carefully at my newly developed body of work and grabbed it on my way out the door. Then, once I got to the club, I shook off all my anxiety and nervousness and pushed my shoulders back like I had been born for that moment. Because I was.

Coco walked me to the back of the club, where Prince was seated at a table with two women I didn't know. As soon as we got close and Coco gave me the signal, I jumped right into my spiel.

"Hi, my name is Kim Berry, and I do hair." I handed the portfolio to Coco, who laid it down in front of Prince. "I also know that you don't have a hairstylist right now."

I struggled to appear calm, hiding my shaky hand behind my back, while Prince flipped through my book. After what felt like hours, he looked up at me with his classic "so what?" expression that has since been turned into a million Internet memes.

"You do hair, huh?" he said, a little too nonchalantly for me.

"Yes, I do."

Prince studied me, raking his eyes over my clothes, and hair, before landing on my face. Nothing got past Prince, so I knew he recognized me. I just needed to know that he was going to give me a chance.

And thank the Lord Almighty, he did.

"Okay," he said. "You got a salon you can go set up?"

"I sure do," I said, not able to get the words out fast enough. I didn't even bother to hide my grin.

Prince was already on to the next, looking past me to another woman who was approaching his table. "Okay, cool," he said. "Set it up, and I'll be there shortly."

I left the club immediately and headed to Simply C.J.'s, a salon in Inglewood where I rented a booth. From watching Tanya, I knew how to set everything up just the way he liked it, including blacking out the windows with sheets and laying out only the right products and tools. I was gassed up on pure adrenaline, barreling through each task at warp speed. Within the hour, everything was perfect. I hadn't been finished for more than five minutes when the phone in the salon rang.

"Kim, this is Prince," the voice said. "I'm not going to be able to get my hair done tonight after all."

It was like a cloud above me had burst from the weight of its water, and the downpour was washing away every bit of hope I'd had of working with the Purple One.

"No problem," I said, willing my heartbeat to slow as I tried valiantly to maintain my composure. "Just know that whenever you're in L.A. you always have a stylist."

There was silence on the other end. I wondered if Prince had already hung up, and I was planning to do the same. Then he spoke again.

"Do you travel?"

Of course I didn't travel. I had never been on a plane. I had never been outside of California. Truth be told, I hadn't been further than the Bay Area! But I didn't tell Prince that.

I let the words flow from my heart, which was filled with the encouragement of my mother and the drive and determination of my father.

"Of course I travel!" I said.

"Good. We're sending a car to pick you up now. The flight leaves in an hour."

It was like he was speaking a foreign language. "What did you just say?"

"Is there a problem?" He sounded confused that I would question him.

But then, so suddenly, the rain was gone and the sunlight was so bright it damn near blinded me.

"No," I said, casually, while frantically shoving everything I had just set up back into my bag. "I'll be ready."

*"Success is when preparedness meets opportunity.
So when the opportunity presents itself,
will you be prepared?"*[9]
—**Mr. Berry (Pops)**

I called my mom right after I got off the phone with Prince. After convincing her that I wasn't making the whole thing up! *That I really was getting on a plane to style the hair of the man behind Purple Rain, Little Red Corvette, 1999, and a dozen other hits!* She prayed and gave me her blessing. I was worried about clothes, and toiletries, since I didn't have time to come home and pack my things! But, she shushed me, promising to wire me some money the next morning so I could get whatever I needed! Telling me not to worry about silly things like that. *What is a toothbrush or a pair of jeans when you're flying out to work with Prince?*

Once I arrived at the airport I discovered that I was headed to Minneapolis - more specifically to Chanhassen, Minnesota,- the suburban home of Prince, and his musical playland, Paisley Park. When we landed I felt like I had been dropped inside one of those toy snow globes. It never rains in southern California; Lord knows it doesn't snow, so Minnesota was a winter wonderland like I had only read about! And when he told me that he preferred being in Chanhassen for the holidays, I completely understood. I learned quickly that Minnesota cold is the kind that creeps up under your clothes and seeps right into your bones. But the sight of falling snowflakes reflected in the glow of millions of tiny, flickering lights was the most beautiful thing I had ever seen.

And, of course, there was Paisley.

When we pulled up to the gates, I remember being in awe—not just at its majesty, but also by the fact that it was actually real! I had heard fans talk about it like it was some mythical castle. Yet, I was right in front of it, seeing it with my own eyes. I wanted a tour, but there was no time for that just yet. As soon as I entered the massive double doors, I was escorted to the salon, where I knew I would soon have my official audition. Prince's brother, Duane Nelson, had been on the flight from L.A. with me. He told me to do his hair first. Then he brought in three women. One by one, I hooked them up. Finally, when the last head was finished, Duane popped back into the salon, told me to have a seat, and said that that he would be back in a few minutes.

I did as I was told. I sat patiently, with my hands folded in my lap, and I waited. And waited. And waited some more. A few minutes turned into thirty, which turned into an hour, until, eventually, two hours had passed.

At that point, it was almost 5:00 in the morning—Christmas morning—and I was getting worried. What if it was all a joke? What if I had made a huge mistake in dropping everything to fly across the country with some men I didn't even know?

Still seated, I looked around the salon and saw the iconic purple coat that Prince had worn in *Purple Rain* and the sky-themed suit he donned in the "Raspberry Beret" video.

They were both hanging on wardrobe racks across the room from me, next to a table covered in rings, necklaces, and other jewelry. Surrounded by mementos from some of the best moments in music history, I had a revelation, and I decided that even if nothing ever came of this opportunity—if I never did Prince's hair, or even talked to him again—I had already had an experience that few others could. And it was worth it.

By the time Duane reappeared I couldn't wait any longer. Literally.

"You didn't steal anything, did you?"

I rolled my eyes as he surveyed the costumes and piles of accessories. "Of course not. I ain't crazy, and my mama didn't raise no fools." I paused, plastered on a smile. "But I am about to pee on myself."

Duane laughed. "Girl, you know you coulda got up and went to the bathroom."

I thought on that for a second and then shook my head. "Nope. I don't just walk around other people's houses like that."

Duane nodded like he understood and showed me to the restroom. When I got back to the salon he once again told me to have a seat, but this time I didn't have to wait for hours. Ten minutes later Prince finally showed up. He smiled and graciously introduced himself as if he were a guest in my home, and not the other way around. I had been mentally preparing, determined to give this man the best hair experience of his life. When I saw him, I had to take a couple deep breaths to keep from forgetting everything I knew. I also took note of how small Prince looked in the salon, far away from a stage or screen, or the multi-colored neon lights of a nightclub. I'd always known he was petite, but under the spell of his mesmerizing music, he'd seemed larger than life.

After our hellos, but before I could ask what he wanted

done with his hair, Prince motioned toward my hands and my long, curved nails. "I'm tender-headed," he said, "so if you're gonna do my hair, you're gonna have to leave those nails at home."

I smiled politely, and without a second thought, I popped those fake nails off one by one.

For a second Prince was just staring, dumbfounded, and I wondered if I'd messed up. Should I have played it cool and taken off my nails later? Then, like a sudden flip had been switched, he bent over and busted out in laughter. "Yeah, you're going to work out perfectly," he said, catching his breath. "Now go get a few hours of sleep. We leave for Miami in the morning."

So there I was, a teenager fresh out of beauty school, away from home for the first time, and about to hit the road with the biggest artist in the world.

After the limo dropped me off and I checked into the hotel, I called my mom. It was 5:00 am California time, and her voice was groggy with sleep. Mine, though, was filled with amazement. I told her everything that had happened—from my first plane ride, to my new manicure, to the Miami trip that was only hours away! I was just so overwhelmed, so in awe of what God had done.

"Mom, who lives like this?" I wondered aloud.

I could hear tears in her voice when she replied, "You do, baby. You do."

Endorphinmachine

PRINCE'S PERSONAL FACIAL PRODUCTS
Those he used to keep "that" face flawless

ORIGINS - CHECKS AND BALANCES
FROTHY FACE WASH

ORIGINS - GINZING ENERGY BOOSTING GEL

OIL OF OLAY MOISTURIZER

PONDS COLD CREAM CLEANSER

COLOR

T HE COLOR OF *traditional diamonds is graded on a scale of D to Z, with "Z" representing an undesirable, light-yellow shade, and "D" distinguishing those diamonds that are perfectly colorless. But in the world of fine jewelry, even "D"-rated stones aren't always the most valuable. Whether blue or orange, red or black, colored diamonds are as natural as their clear counterparts, yet they are rare and vivid, uniquely attractive and, often, highly coveted.*

I will never forget the first time one of the looks I created for Prince went viral. We didn't call it viral back then, of course. We just knew that everywhere we went, from concerts to airports, there were a slew of Prince lookalikes. It was as if women from across the country, of all ages and backgrounds, had studied Prince's most recent photos and album art and then determined that wearing the same hairstyle he did made them the most worthy of all his fans.

The year was 1999, and it was just before the release of Prince's *Rave Un2 the Joy Fantastic*. He was still the Artist Formerly Known as Prince then, and the album was his first Arista release, following the final fulfillment of his contractual obligations with Warner Brothers. And, as always, a new project meant a new look.

People often ask me how Prince and I came up with certain hairstyles. Were they his ideas or mine? Or, do we get the ideas from some third-party source? But it's impossible for me to pinpoint the source of Prince's inspiration because it really came from everywhere. Often, because Prince wanted to be aware of what people were doing, especially overseas, I'd bring in pictures from the Paris, and Milan fashions shows, and rip pages from *Vogue,* and other fashion magazines. Prince knew that the U.S. was always just a step behind. A tad bit late. But he never copied anything he saw verbatim. Like with his music, Prince's intention with his personal style was to *set* trends, not to follow them. If the rest of the world was long, Prince wanted to go short. If everyone else was wearing their hair straight, he wanted to rock curls. Truthfully, that determination to go against the grain was probably the main reason he wore so many female hairstyles. People called him feminine and questioned his sexuality, but really, he was just setting himself apart. Doing what no other male singer would dare to do.

Once Prince finally decided on a style that he could commit to for the duration of an album cycle, he gave me the command, and I got to work making it happen. I'd put my Kim Berry spin on it, always staying true to his vision but letting my creativity shine through, too. And let me tell you— we did some fun stuff over the years. Prince rocked Ombre way before it was called Ombre; I hooked him up with an edgy short cut when Rhianna was still a baby. In fact, Prince used to jokingly wonder why Halle Berry got all the shine for her cute pixie—leading people to refer to the style as the "Halle Berry cut"—when he wore it first, and in his opinion, better.

> *"Prince was a diamond of matchless beauty, that everywhere light struck him, a color emitted from his being."*[10]
>
> —**Minister Louis Farrakhan**

But back to the style that spawned a million lookalikes.

It was the eve of the release of *Rave Un2 the Joy Fantastic,* and just months shy of the new millennium, and Prince and I were walking through Paisley, having an impromptu photo shoot. In addition to putting out some of the hottest music ever recorded, Prince's job was to make sure that everybody at Paisley stayed busy. No standing around, no sitting and talking to other staff. Prince wanted everybody working at all times, so when he saw that his photographer, Steve Parke, was just walking around aimlessly, with nothing to do, Prince grabbed him by his arm, looked at me, and said, "Let's make magic happen."

On that day, "magic" meant "new pictures." So Prince, Steve, and I started walking around the building, looking for the perfect spot to snap some photos. I had already done his hair, but I tagged along, just in case Prince needed something along the way. Turns out he did. We were in the atrium, just outside the kitchen, when Prince turned to me and said, "Kim, I want some braids.

Prince's hair had been short for *Crystal Ball* and mid-length in the artwork for *The Vault: Old Friends 4 Sale*. It was his last album for Warner Brothers that had been released just month's prior. In between projects I was either cutting Prince's hair, or growing it out. At this time it was long, hanging just shy of his shoulders. I already had it feathered and beautiful, so I was confused by his request.

"Just braid it up," he repeated.

I immediately thought he had lost his mind, but I wasn't going to tell him that, of course. "Um, I don't know what you mean," I said. "You want cornrows, or?"

He waved his hand, interrupting me. "No. Not cornrows! Just take big sections all over my head and braid them. My cousin used to wear her hair like that, and that's what I want, so hook me up!"

I took a deep breath and nodded. "You got it."

I kept a set bag on me like bullets for a gun, locked, loaded, and always ready to fire. I opened it up, grabbed a chair for him to sit in, and immediately went to work. I parted a two-inch section and wove it into a quick braid; the kind little girls wear with primary-colored baubles and bows. Then I held up a hand mirror in front of the braid so he could see it in the reflection.

He smiled. "That's perfect. That's exactly what I want."

Steve was standing idly as he waited for me to finish the

look when Prince joked, "I should have Steve take a picture of you braiding my hair."

"Yeah, you should," I said, half-listening, and before I got the words out of my mouth, Steve had already started snapping, documenting a little piece of history that has since been shared on the internet countless times.

Meanwhile, I kept working until his head was covered in a dozen thin braids. When I finished, I stood still as he stared at his reflection in the mirror. I didn't say anything, didn't try to dissuade him from this foolishness. I just waited on him to change his mind, to tell me to undo them and to grab the curling iron. Instead he just kept right on smiling at himself.

"I guess all you need now is some barrettes," I said.

I was being sarcastic, but when I met Prince's eyes, they were wide like saucers. "No, not barrettes—I have an even better idea! Go upstairs to wardrobe and bring me some leftover fabric from the suit I'm wearing."

I shook my head, flabbergasted! I thought about my mom, who would put similar braids in my hair so she wouldn't have to comb it for a week. Prince was notoriously tender-headed and would do whatever he could to extend a hairstyle and avoid having to sit in my chair. The less pulling and tugging I had to do, the happier he was. But this was too much! Again, though, I knew better than to say anything. When Prince wanted what he wanted, you either did it for him or you didn't. And if you didn't, he would just do it himself. You, meanwhile, would be sitting up looking crazy—and you'd be doing it *outside* the Paisley gates.

Paisley was designed so that Prince would never have to leave the premises if he didn't want to. He had everything he needed inside those walls, including an entire wardrobe department with designers, tailors, and racks and racks of clothes. There was an assumption that famous high-end designers like Versace and Dolce & Gabbana would dress an artist of Prince's magnitude. Yet, even though he did have a few designer pieces here and there, the vast majority of Prince's closet was custom-designed by amazingly talented people who no one had ever heard of. Prince had a crazy knack for finding talent, and would turn over any rock to find the people who were the absolute best in their fields. He'd reach out to people he saw on YouTube, or start conversations with folks he met on tour, and no matter where they were from, or what their background was, if they were good, he'd hire them on the spot.

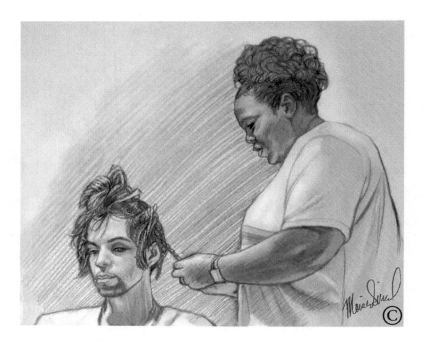

Debbie is an artist extraordinaire from the south side of Chicago who designed all of Prince's clothing. She was a quiet soul, but a force to be reckoned with when it came to designing, and could stand toe-to-toe with any major designer. Her heart and her loyalty kept Prince fly for over a decade. A lot of the promotional artwork that was created—from the NPG Music Club website, to the *20Ten* album cover—Debbie created. Debbie and I had each other's backs! Even though we cried, when we needed to, we spent most of our time laughing and cracking jokes about our crazy, exhausting, exhilarating lives—lives that no one outside of the Prince camp would even believe! We had our trusty Motorola pagers (that were eventually upgraded to sidekicks) to keep us abreast on whatever Prince needed, whether it was a hat, some cuff links, or hair gel. Hell, because I was often the one standing next to Prince before he went on stage, he would tell me that he needed a hem in his pants. And sometimes Debbie was the one to take over hair and makeup, while I tightened things up in the wardrobe department. We all had multiple jobs. The bottom line was that we were to do whatever was necessary to get that man to the stage.

As for me, Prince loved bragging to people about his "home girl from Compton" even though I wasn't from Compton at all. Later, after he'd introduced me to someone, I'd pull him to the side and remind him that I was actually from Inglewood, but he'd shush me, saying that his little fib just added to the mystery. He loved the idea of finding people before anyone else did! And, as long as you could meet his standards of excellence, he would put you on. It was up to you how long you stayed on. And while Prince certainly did his fair share of firing, most of the people who cycled in and out of his camp had fired themselves.

. Tunic with a combination of concha's buttons & Buttons (in silver tone or Gold tone) with some of the concha's having flat thin piping weaved through to create some fringe detail

. (All light weight concha's & Buttons)

scarf fabric sample is in an ombre fabric, could also be in any print too, or scarf in main fabric & the underside in another color and or print.

After Prince's ribbon revelation, I was off to the wardrobe department, already laughing at the dumbstruck response I was sure to get from the design team. I pushed the door open, stumbled in, and yelled, "Quick! I need ribbons for Prince!"

Sure enough, Debbie and Bonnie, one of the tailors, were completely confused. But every wish out of Prince's mind was our command, so when I explained that I needed leftover fabric from his suit, and that I would need fabric from every new suit until further notice, they obliged. Just another case of Paisley magic at its best!

I returned to the atrium, fabric in hand, and began cutting it into thin strips. When I was finished, I wove a piece of ribbon around each braid, going about halfway up. The whole time I was doing it, I just knew that he'd change his mind and this would be one of those throwaway styles that years later we'd look back at and crack up thinking about the crazy Technicolor braids! But that's not what happened. Prince loved the style so much that it became the cover look for *Rave Un2 The Joy Fantastic*. Amazingly, it also became a style that women around the country began copying, dividing their hair into Buckwheat braids and wrapping them in colorful fabric.

> "*It's all good when U know the only fame*
> *Is the light that comes from God*
> *& the joy U get 2 say His name*"[11]
>
> —**From the song "Don't Play Me" by Prince**

The first time I saw a handful of these Prince lookalikes, I busted out laughing. Surely, they hadn't looked in the mirror on their way out the door. I mean it couldn't possibly have been their intention to look like grown-up six-year-olds? But Prince just shrugged and said, "I told you so, Kim." As if he knew when he came up with the style, on a whim, that everyone would clamor to duplicate.

That was typical Prince. Regardless of any apprehension we may have had about a new stylistic direction, Prince exuded certainty. Forever confident that the creative decisions he made would shatter molds, and be well received by fans. Our process was a collaborative one, and he looked to me, as well as the other members of his glam squad, to share opinions and contribute to the overall look. Ultimately, though, the final decisions were his, and his alone.

Our job was to be ready at all times, to execute whatever crazy idea popped into his beautiful, strange mind.

Thankfully, I'd had the perfect training.

The rules at Pacific Beauty School were made clear from day one:

Class started at 8:00. If you showed up at 8:01 you were getting locked out of the building. If you showed up with a dirty smock or dirty shoes, you were getting sent home. And if you missed a day, you couldn't come back for thirty more.

Mr. Goines was serious about educating us and he played no games. He knew that, for black women, the road to success would be riddled with potholes and oil slicks. He also knew that having a practical skill that was always in demand would give us the financial security that many black families were still struggling to achieve. He was like equal parts teacher and life coach. Every time he taught us a new lesson, I flashed back to Mr. Miyagi in *The Karate Kid*, instructing Daniel to wax on and wax off. Reinforcing the virtual habits that would turn into real life skills.

Mr. Goines' stern, no-nonsense demeanor was too much for some of the other girls, but I was used to it. My mom didn't play either, so the rules and guidelines at Pacific, while tough, were nothing I was afraid of. Expectations were high, and as I discovered later, they provided the professional foundation that I would repeatedly lean on once I became Prince's personal hairstylist. But Mr. Goines had no way of knowing that some of us would later become celebrity hairstylists, working with multiplatinum artists, and award-winning actors. He was simply focused on turning us all into the best hairstylists possible, and he shared that load with our primary instructor, Ms. Cooper.

I showed up at the school each morning by 7:30, 7:45 at the latest. My smock and shoes were sparkling, and I was always equipped with a swift yes ma'am and no sir. My home training made it easy for me to fly under the radars of Mr. Goines and Ms. Cooper, but even if I hadn't been preconditioned to follow the rules, there was another student who gave me all the incentive I needed to stay on the right track. Pat.

Pat had been attending Pacific for four years—despite the fact that it was a one-year program. She had taken multiple breaks; she'd had a baby; she had done just about everything *but* finish beauty school! One day I even asked her: "You know this is not regular college, right?"

It didn't take me long to decide I was going to be the exact opposite of Pat. But even though I was showing up on time every day, and following all the rules, I was still just going through the motions, trying to get through the year as quickly as possible without really giving my all to the program. Ms. Cooper noticed, and she wasn't happy about it.

"I'll show you fat meat is greasy."[12]

—**Mr. Berry (Pops)**

"Why are you here?" she asked me one morning.

I plastered on a smile. "I'm here because my mother made me come."

"Oh, so you don't want to do hair?"

I thought about how to respond and decided there was no reason to lie. "No, I don't" I said, flatly. "I'm going to college next year, and I'm going to be a doctor. My mom just didn't want me sitting at home in the meantime. So, I'm gonna go ahead and get through this program."

"Oh, I see," Ms. Cooper said, peering over the top of her glasses. "That sounds like a good plan. But just so you know, by the end of this course, I'm going to turn you into a hairstylist."

I crossed my arms defiantly. "No, you're not."

She laughed—one of those annoying, *I don't care what you say because I'm not even listening* laughs. "Oh, yes," she said. "Yes, I am."

With Pat's image embedded in brain, I kept pushing myself. I stayed in the books, determined to learn every new concept as quickly as possible. Along the way I realized I had a knack for hairstyling, and I was progressing faster than some of the other girls. Ms. Cooper saw this, too (she saw *everything*), and one day she decided to put my knowledge to the test by sending me out to the floor. Had it been a regular Friday in the middle of February or June, I might have been okay, and maybe not so nervous. But it was the Friday before Easter, and we were overflowing with women, and girls, expecting to get their hair *laid* for the celebration of Jesus' resurrection.

Like at all beauty schools, the general public could book hair appointments at Pacific. We were students, so it gave us some real-world, hands-on experience, and because we weren't yet professionals, our rates were much cheaper than those of standard salons. It was a win-win. Now, students at Pacific typically had to have worked through a certain number of courses before they could go out on the floor. But on that day, with the Easter crowd swelling, and some of the more experienced students out sick, Ms. Cooper had to pull one of the new girls.

"Berry," she said, tapping my shoulder, "it's time."

She pointed in the direction of my client, a petite, elderly woman who wanted her hair curled. My stomach was knotting, and while I knew the material in the books front and back, working on a real, live person was another thing altogether. I didn't feel ready, but if Ms. Cooper said I was, I had to at least fake it. I walked over to the woman, introduced myself, and started working. I was talking to myself, trying not to let my nerves get the best of me, but it didn't work. I mistakenly got the curling iron too hot, and as soon as I wrapped the barrel around the woman's hair, it burned an entire curl right off her head. She might as well have been completely bald cause, for a moment, all I could do was stand there in shock. I was trying to come up with a plan. Some strategy to hide my sin, but I couldn't think fast enough. I turned around and Ms. Cooper was standing right behind me, her expression stern and cold.

I don't know whether Ms. Cooper smelled the funk of burned hair, or saw the look of terror on my face, but she asked me flat-out, "Did you burn this lady's hair?"

I panicked. I didn't want to lie, but I saw no other solution. "No," I said, stealthily placing the singed curl in my pocket. I didn't want Ms. Cooper to see it, but I also needed to hide my mistake from some of the more seasoned stylists on the floor. They would have definitely clowned me if they knew that I couldn't even do a simple press and curl.

"Kim, I'm going to ask you again," Ms. Cooper pressed. "Did you burn this lady's hair?"

I repeated the lie, but Ms. Cooper wasn't convinced. Doing

what any good teacher would do, she pushed me to the side, grabbed a comb, and started raking through the woman's hair. I think I held my breath the whole time, waiting to just pass out on the floor, but it didn't take long for her to find the exact spot of the missing curl. I was expecting her to yell at me, to kick me out, or *something*! Instead, she remained eerily calm.

"The next time I ask you if you've burned someone, you need to admit it," she said. "The clients know you're a beauty school student, and this is the chance that they take in coming here." I said nothing. I just stood there with my head down, trying to hide the embarrassment that was flooding my face. When she was finished, I turned to walk away and started untying my apron. I didn't get far before Ms. Cooper grabbed my arm and pulled me back behind the chair. "What are you doing?" she snapped. "You need to get back to work and finish your client's hair!" I was terrified, but once again, I had no other option. Ms. Cooper placed the curling iron in my hand and stood, waiting, until I picked up where I had left off, carefully positioning the poor lady's remaining curls so that they would cover the space left empty by my amateur mistake. Once I finished I was finally able to walk off the floor, heading back to the comfort of books and mannequins. I wasn't sure if I would ever be able to forgive myself for burning that woman's hair and be able to work on a live person again, but there was no wallowing in self-pity at Pacific. Just a few weeks later, I had an opportunity to redeem myself.

Ms. Cooper came in on a Monday morning and announced that we would all be participating in a mandatory, two-day hair competition. 200 kids were coming in from all over the state to compete, and the winner would receive a cash prize. We had four days to find a model and get ready before the contest commenced.

The burned curl was still fresh in my mind, so I wasn't sure if I wanted to participate in the competition, let alone try to win. But I was damn sure gonna try. First things first, I called my home girl, Marna, and asked her if she would be my model. Her mother had bought her about eight different prom dresses, and when Marna said yes, she agreed to wear one of them. Meanwhile, my wheels started spinning on her hairstyle. Even though Marna's hair was very long, she agreed to let me cut it—and this was way before the super short, Anita Baker look was popular. We were already taking a chance with the cut, but Marna said she was also down to let me add a little bit of color for some extra pop.

Bishop Ervin used to say, "If you don't see it before you see it; you'll never see it. The vision is the boss." Now, I could see what I wanted Marna's hair to look like in my mind; the problem was that I was having a really hard time executing what I envisioned. When I added the color, Marna's hair came out pink. Then it turned a nasty shade of green before finally settling into a burnt orange hue. Marna looked so terrible that I started working on my speech. I knew I would need to have something prepared when I told my mom I had flunked out of beauty school.

In one last ditch effort, I asked Ms. Cooper for help. I figured she was probably still pissed at me for burning the woman's hair before Easter, but I also thought she'd be willing to do it for Marna's sake, even if she didn't want to help me. Surprisingly, Ms. Cooper flat-out said no. She didn't budge either, just told me to go back to my books and figure it out. It was in that moment that I became convinced she was trying to sabotage me. I'd watched her sauntering about, assisting the other competitors in my class, and my mouth dropped as she walked away and left me standing in my tracks.

Ms. Cooper had already put me on the floor too soon, and now she wouldn't help me fix my home girl's hair. Marna's hair looked like an orangutan's fur! Despite the fact that she was helping everyone else, instead of assisting me, Ms. Cooper was happy to watch me flounder! For some of the girls, she was outright doing their heads! Yet, instead of discouraging me, something about Ms. Cooper's refusal to help pushed me forward. It was like a switch had been flipped, and with no other choice, I went back and studied how to color correct. Then I experimented, and tweaked Marna's hair until it was perfect. The day of the competition she came out in a black, floor-length, velvet gown that she had paired with long, rhinestone-studded gloves. Marna looked like an actual model. I felt so proud of myself for not giving up when things had gotten so hard. I would remember this, years later, each time I called my mom after Prince had upset me again. Or when there had been another incident on the road, and I was *convinced* that I was going to quit! "Winners don't quit, and quitters never win!" my mom would say before praying with me.

I didn't quit the beauty competition, and in the first day's qualifying round, I finished in the top 10 out of 200 people. On the second day, I came back and grabbed the top spot! As I was collecting my trophy, and $500 check, from Ms. Cooper, she leaned in and whispered, "Didn't I tell you I would turn you into a hair stylist?"

As much as I hated to admit it, she was right. I had fought my way through that competition and come out with the top look! If that wasn't God's work, I don't know what it was. With the check clutched tightly in my hand, I had to think; maybe I really *am* a hairstylist? That realization drove me to commit to the process more than before, but it certainly didn't make things easier. If winning the competition had lit a fire under me, making the declaration that I would do hair for a living added gasoline right on top of the flame.

Once the other girls and I hit the floor and started working with outside clientele on a regular basis, we were given a bundle of towels each morning. Each towel had a slip of paper bearing the name of a client wrapped around it. Each client needed his or her hair to be shampooed and dried, before moving on to styling. Each morning I watched as Mr. Goines, who oversaw the salon part of the school, handed the other girls one or two towels. Inevitably, he'd hand me a stack of six! This happened day after day, for weeks on end. Until, finally, I couldn't take it anymore! I was sick of him playing favorites; sick of him trying to make a fool of me, like Ms. Cooper had tried to. "Wait a minute," I said. "This isn't fair! Why do I always have to take on more clients than the other girls?"

I was frustrated and distraught, but Mr. Goines completely ignored my question. "Berry," he said, "when I come back in an hour, I need all these tickets shampooed, conditioned, blow dried, and ready to be curled. Do you understand me?"

I started to protest again, but I stopped short as I began to recognize what was happening. It was another opportunity for me, another chance to meet a challenge and rise above it, to prepare for my destiny. I got all those heads shampooed and dried within the hour, and when Mr. Goines came back, he nodded. I was expecting some praise, maybe a congratulations. But Mr. Goines' expectations for me were so high that he didn't consider my work extraordinary.

He checked each head, and said, "Good work, Berry" then added, "Just remember, it's more important to be good than fast. Quality and *then* quantity! Never sacrificing one for the other. You don't want to be the stylist that has customers come in first thing in the morning and they're still in your chair till late in the afternoon."

He was right, of course. Being forced to prep so many heads so quickly—and do it well—gave me the speed that I needed to succeed in the entertainment industry. Whether you're on the set of a music video or a feature film, time is money. And if a director ever has to wait on you to finish someone's hair before he can start shooting again, you might as well start looking for a new job.

Ms. Cooper and Mr. Goines pushed me so hard that I pushed myself right through beauty school in nine months instead of 12. I remember thinking that I wanted to finish as quickly as possible because I wanted to get out from underneath their thumbs, but really, I was just operating in God's perfect timing. It wasn't long after I finished that my opportunity to take Tanya's place as Prince's stylist suddenly appeared.

I thought back to those stacks of towels when I first arrived at Paisley and was instructed to style four people, back-to-back, for my audition. I had been training with heavy weights since beauty school, so whipping through those heads was light work. If I ever made a mistake or tried something that failed, I would think back to that little woman with the missing curl, and I would blanket myself in the grace that she and Ms. Cooper showed, knowing that I could always recover. And whenever Prince was ready to change up his look—whether he wanted to rock a pompadour ponytail or a head full of braids—I thought about the hair competition and felt confident that my skills were the best in the game.

Enlightened human beings can be created by great teachers, and because of Ms. Cooper and Mr. Goines, I was one who was set apart in this elite industry.

Endorphinmachine

Moisture is a Must In Producing a Mirror Like Shine
Hair Must Be As Poppin' as Your Highlighter

ARGON'S HOT OIL TREATMENT

COCONUT OIL MIXED WITH YOUR FAVORITE MOISTURIZER

MOTIONS

ULTIMATE TRIPLE SILK

NEXUS HUMECTRESS

GINA RIVERA BIOGEN COMPLEX
REJUVENATING CONDITIONER

CLARITY

A DIAMOND'S CLARITY IS *based on its number of imperfections, and all diamonds have some. They may be hidden or invisible to the naked eye, but on closer inspection, especially when magnified, these imperfections are always revealed. The good news is that clarity can be improved upon. By re-cutting, and re-polishing, the stone to remove unsightly inclusions a greater reflection of light occurs.*

Prince didn't find God the way a lot of us did. His parents didn't drag him out of bed early Sunday morning and then, once his hair was brushed and his skin was slathered with Vaseline, slam him into a church pew. He didn't attend Sunday school, 11:00 a.m. worship, the 3:00 p.m. afternoon service, and Wednesday night prayer meeting every week, week after week, until the gospel became a familiar refrain. A soundtrack studded with the Clark Sisters, and Shirley Caesar, that played on incessant loop.

That was certainly my story, though. At my house, Sunday was the Lord's Day, and it wasn't even a question whether we'd be up bright and early, sliding into our church clothes. As my brothers got older, they tended to do what teenage boys do, making up their own minds and ignoring grown folks, and more often than not, that meant they didn't go to church. But I, being the only girl, I was always under my mother's rule. When friends came over to spend the night on Saturdays, I was instructed to tell them in advance: Bring some nice clothes cause we're going to church in the morning. And sure enough, no matter how late we'd stayed up gossiping or listening to music, my mom would bust into the room at the first sign of daylight, pushing open curtains and pulling back covers, yanking everybody out of their deep sleep so we wouldn't be late.

I was baptized when I was six years old, and over the years I spent more hours listening to preaching and teaching than I could ever count. But just being in church every week wasn't enough for me to develop my relationship with Him that I now rely on as an adult. The old church ladies used to say that in order to follow God, you have to know Him for yourself. You could only follow your mother's God, or your father's God for so long—soon enough you have to develop your own faith. I didn't understand what they meant back then, but as I got older, transitioning from childhood to young adulthood, it all became clear that it's not about religion, it's about relationship.

"It is during our darkest moments that we must focus to see the light" [13]
— **Aristotle**

I grew up in L.A. "east of the 110" in the 80s, when crack hit the streets and black household incomes hit the skids. Back then - same as now- everybody needed a savior. Some folks found it on the corner, or at the bottom of a bottle, but I turned to God. Lying in bed at night, I could hear my mother's sobs through the thin walls of our house as she cried out to Jesus. She would be begging, pleading with God to provide, to keep us safe! To bless this person or that person! And He answered every prayer. I knew that instinctively because, even as danger inched closer and closer, I was always spared.

In my community, gang banging and dope dealing was

as common as fried chicken and toilet paper. All the neighborhood boys wanted to be that dude in the fancy car with the bumpin' sounds, and nobody wanted to find a safe (or legal) way to get there. But when you live by the streets, you die by the streets, so it was nothing to see our friends get gunned down, or to hear over breakfast that so-and-so's son had gotten jumped the night before. It was life in the big city, and I knew that my survival, my ability to meet each new day with health and strength, was a testament to God's grace and protection.

After years of listening to my mother's prayers, I began to feel the urge to talk to God myself. I no longer wanted to rely on my mother interceding for me, or explaining a scripture so I could understand it. I just started dropping to my knees and reaching out to Him on my own. I also began studying my Bible, along with every self-help book and inspirational memoir I could find, thinking they held all the secrets to the good life. In my mind, they did. Eventually, I was waking myself up on Sunday mornings, already dressed before my mother even came into my room.

That's not to say that I was perfect or without flaws! I was still young, so I did plenty of dumb stuff and made more mistakes than I probably should have. But I also knew I was special. I knew I was set apart and destined for greatness, and seeing a couple of my brothers who were always running the streets and in constant trouble, it was even more incentive to stay on the straight and narrow.

Once, in high school, my friends had ditched school and were headed to McDonald's. I wanted to go, too, but I wasn't about to sneak out and risk getting in trouble. My solution was to ask for a hall pass from the principal, and because I was a good kid and kept my nose clean, he gave me permission to leave school during lunch, giving me the chance to meet up with my friends. By the time I got to the restaurant, they were already there, laughing and joking, oblivious to the conse-quences that lay ahead. Sure enough, it was only minutes later when a truancy officer strolled in the front door and started taking everybody's name and number. Meanwhile, I showed the officer my principal's note and walked right out of there with my cheeseburger and a clean record.

As I got older, the crimes my friends committed got more serious. Some of my girlfriends started hanging with older boys, sneaking out to go drink and have sex. I'd be lying if I said I didn't go along with them sometimes, or sneak out on my own to go spend time with Coco. But, when I did, I was careful not to do any of the things my friends were doing. Even if everybody in the room was smoking weed. I'd take the joint and pass it right over to the next person without even thinking about taking a hit.

My logic was simple:

I knew my mother was strict as hell and wouldn't hesitate to whoop my behind in the middle of the street if I even looked like I was about to do something crazy.

My objective was to never, ever, *ever* disappoint my father.

My dad used to tell me, "A man ain't got nothing in this world but his word and his black ass! So, if your word don't mean nothing, what I'mma do with the rest of you?"

I took that to heart and wore my integrity like a crown. I kept my word and was always there for friend or foe. I was taught to do unto others as you would have them do unto you, and I never once strayed from that principle. Most importantly, I was committed to following the teachings that my father, and especially my mother, laid out before me. If my mother told me to do something, I did it. And if she told me not to do something... Well, it wouldn't matter how much I *wanted* to, because I couldn't bring myself to actually do it.

My mother told me to go to school, get good grades, and bring home a diploma, so I did. She told me to never bring a baby into her house, and I didn't, even when it meant making one of the most difficult decisions of my life.

It took me years to understand that my mother wasn't mean for the sake of being mean. Only when I became an adult, and had my own child, did I understand that she truly had my best interest in mind. And, when I think back to my girlfriends who were getting pregnant and having babies in junior high and even elementary school, I feel grateful for her wisdom that I now know saved me from so much earthly pain. For so long I thought I was hearing the voice of my mother, keeping me right when it was so easy to go left, but it wasn't hers. The voice that was constantly playing in my head was God's! And, I needed to hear it more than ever when I went to work for Prince.

> *"You can depend on God to see you through, and you can depend on me to pray for you."*[14]
> — **Bishop Paul S. Morton**

Prince's biological parents were Seventh Day Adventists, but they didn't take him to weekly meetings on a regular basis. As a result, Prince didn't relate to organized religious demonstrations as a child. There was the music of course, and the sounds of the choir stroked the creative spark first lit by his father's jazz performances in Minneapolis nightclubs. But, Prince had to find his own way to God, and it took him a little while.

That's not to say that Prince wasn't always spiritual. On the contrary, he was wise beyond his years and told me that he always had a relationship with God, even as a boy. Prince knew from an early age that he was a vessel created by God to bring music into the world. And, he frequently spoke about the moment when that prophetic Word was dropped into his spirit. As it turned out, that wasn't the only prophecy Prince received as a child.

In a 2009 interview with Tavis Smiley, Prince said that he had been born epileptic and that the regular seizures he suffered made life difficult for himself and his family. His parents, already struggling financially, didn't know how to accommodate his medial issues, and friends and classmates bullied him at school. Then, suddenly, almost as quickly as they had arrived, the seizures were gone. Prince said that he walked into his mother's room and told her point-blank that he wasn't going to be sick anymore. When she asked him how he could be so sure, he said, simply, "Because an angel told me so."

Like all of us, Prince had a Divine connection from birth. Each of our assignments are given to us before we are born; in fact, the Bible says that before we were formed in our mother's womb He knew us. It's just a matter of us realizing it and stepping out into God's will for our lives. We can then be assured that, when we do, He will always be there to guide us. (As the saying goes, when the student is ready, the teacher will answer.) Prince had enough direct experiences with God to confirm every supernatural gifting, as well as everything he felt in his spirit about his life's purpose. But when I embarked on my journey with him on Christmas Eve in 1988, he wasn't thinking about God at all.

It wasn't at all that surprising, honestly. Prince was riding high from the success of *Purple Rain* and *1999*, getting ready for *Batman*, and just a couple years away from *Diamonds and Pearls*. Basically, he was on top of the world. That seems like an amazing position to be in; especially if you believe that the definition of success is having access to anything you want, anytime you want it. But as Biggie said, "mo' money brings mo' problems", and having the world at your feet can be difficult to deal with.

When I first started working with him, Prince was still coming to terms with his success while also dealing the residual strife from decades of family issues. He was bigger than life, with chart-topping records and millions of fans, yet he didn't have family support to fall back on. Instead, he built a crew who could keep him grounded, and whom he trusted—sometimes to a fault. On top of that, he was no longer "normal" enough to just walk through the mall, or run to the grocery store, without being mobbed by fans (unless he was in Chanhassen, where people generally left him alone). As a result, Prince handled his fame the only way he knew how—by living wild and free, with no obligations, and no one to answer to. I wasn't in a position to judge ("judge not, lest you be judged"), but I knew that Prince didn't always make the best decisions, especially regarding his treatment of others.

Prince was a taskmaster, and hard on everybody. He was hard on himself, working crazy hours and going nonstop. But, while he could handle the pressure, not everyone could. He'd spend all day and all night in the studio creating new music. Then he'd come out and spend hours teaching the brand new music to the band members, one by one, part by part. They were all great musicians in their own right, but Prince wanted them to be even better. If they made even the slightest mistake, there was hell to pay. Come in a beat too late, or too early - hit a wrong chord - or play in the wrong key, and the musicians already knew their check was going to be $500 lighter. Honestly, docking pay was probably the lightest of punishments; especially since some of the musicians made up to $10,000 each week. Other times Prince would exact discipline by extending rehearsals for hours, or even firing people on the spot.

He yelled and he snapped. And in the early days, before he became a Jehovah's Witness, he cussed people out, degrading and diminishing their hard work without a second thought. Prince knew how he wanted his ship ran, and you either got with the program or you didn't. If you ever ran afoul of his program, and didn't politely see your way out, he'd have you thrown out. But maybe, if you were "lucky," he'd bring in your replacement and have you train them on your way out the door.

Prince tried that mess with me, shortly after he married his second wife, Manuela Testolini. When Manuela showed up at Paisley, she wanted to mark her territory, trying to change things that had been in place for years just so she could put her name on them. There were many areas she could have tackled as the new wife, but I guess she decided that Prince's hairstylist was the best place to start.

Throughout my time working with Prince, many of the women in his life questioned me, and my relationship with him. Deep down they took issue with the fact that I had been around longer than they had, and I would still be around after they were gone. Manuela and I never really hit it off, and it didn't matter to me. I kept my head down and did my work, paying no attention to any sideways glances coming from her. All bets were off, though, when she flew in her personal hairstylist, from New York, and tried to convince Prince to fire me, and hire him. Saturo, the stylist, had flown out twice to cut Prince's hair. He and Prince weren't really feeling each other, but Manuela kept pushing until Prince brought him out a third time. That time, Prince asked me to show him how to do a relaxer. As soon as those words came out of his mouth, I knew what time it was. Why would I teach that man how to do a relaxer when all he ever did was cut Prince's hair? Not only did I refuse, but I also let Saturo in on Prince's scheme.

Up to that point, Prince's ploy of parading someone's

replacement right in front of them only worked because the new person Prince brought in was always willing to do anything to work with him—even if that meant stabbing the current employee in the back. As a result, Prince never considered that someone would actually reject his offer to work for him, but that was exactly what happened with Saturo. Saturo was a high-powered stylist from the Oribe Salon NYC pulling down $5,000 a day. It made zero sense for him to give up his flexible schedule to make less money working full-time for Prince, no matter how many records he had sold.

On his way out the door, after refusing to join Prince's team and still being paid his full $5,000 fee just for trimming Prince's ends, Saturo looked at Prince and said, nonchalantly, "Nobody makes your hair look like Kim does. Why would you even want to replace her?"

Prince never responded. He just turned and looked at Manuela, letting her know that was the end of that, and I wasn't going anywhere.

Unfortunately, those kinds of situations weren't uncommon in the Prince camp. He thrived on playing games and manipulating people, and because we needed our jobs, we dealt with it. My daddy would say, "If Prince says 'Jump,' the people say, 'How high?' And if he says 'Shit,' they squat and say, 'What color?'"

Pops was right. Prince was in complete control of the Monopoly board, playing chess while everybody else played checkers, and he knew it. Aside from his main staff, people on the outside wanted so badly to be in Prince's presence, to rub up against greatness, that they would do whatever he asked them to, even if it was against their better judgement. I saw Prince pull women into threesomes who I know weren't into that, but they also weren't going to pass up an intimate experience with Prince. And there were other women he sent out to recruit the women he wanted to bring back to Paisley, or to his hotel room, for the evening. No matter what he asked for, and of whom he asked it, Prince was always met with a chorus of yeses.

Prince had a lot of respect for me, so he didn't ask me to do anything crazy. I also learned to stay out of his line of fire so we wouldn't have any problems. I did whatever he needed to ensure that he could get on stage each night and wow the fans. No one had just one job in Prince's camp, so in addition to keeping his hair fly; I was also a gopher, a foo-foo girl, a stagehand, a cook, and a cleanup woman. Fetching this, getting that… I labeled myself a glorified babysitter because it was my job to take care of his day-to-day needs. If we were in Belgium and he wanted a certain soap or manicure kit, I had to make my rounds to the local shops, speaking not a word of Dutch, French, or German, and find everything he asked for. Once, in Berlin, I even had to be Prince's pseudo-bodyguard because he had recently fired his whole security team. After that, he decided since God was taking care of him he didn't need security. He had me, and a couple other girls traveling with him, booking cars, advancing the venues, setting up his hotel room, etc., and all I could do was pray that nothing would happen to him before he came to his senses, and hired some real bodyguards.

Going above and beyond kept *me* above the fray, but I still noticed when Prince was dogging someone else out. Any time something went down, I called my mother back in L.A. and told her that there had been another incident, that I didn't know how much more I could take. And every time, no matter what Prince had done, my mother gave him the benefit of the doubt. She tried to understand his motives and emotions, so she could get to the root of whatever led him to mistreat people the way he sometimes did. My mother was a *rida*, and she had lived and seen much more than I had. She knew that sometimes people behaved out of character and did, and said, things they probably shouldn't have. Even from afar, she treated Prince like one of her children, always covering him with love and mercy. Most importantly, though, she prayed for him. She prayed for all of us, really, and her prayers were fervent. As soon as I would start to tell her what drama had gone down at Paisley that day, or who had gotten fired in the middle of a tour, she'd stop me and say, "Okay, let's pray about it. Don't tell me nothing else, let's just pray." And we would immediately go into prayer, right there on the phone.

I know Prince felt those prayers. We often talked about how my mom and I were lifting him up before God, sometimes on a daily basis. I didn't tell him that to make him feel bad or to try to convict him. I just wanted him to know that we loved and cared for him like family. Prince's own family was so disconnected, so he admired the relationship I had with my mom, as well as her devout faith. He joked that she talked to God so much that He was on speed dial, and always expecting her call, answering her prayers like, "Oh. It's you again, Joanne? What do you need now?"

These conversations gave way to longer, more in-depth discussions about God, and with each one, Prince's heart began to soften. But even though our talks helped him draw closer to God, nothing impacted Prince's spiritual life as much as his relationship with Larry Graham.

Larry Graham is a world-renowned bassist who played with Sly and the Family Stone before founding the funk band, Graham Central Station. Prince had admired Larry's musicianship for years, and as he did with all the other musicians he respected, Prince figured out a way to work with him. Ultimately, Larry moved to Minneapolis, with his wife and daughter, and became Prince's new bassist. All the while, Prince keep him close, letting Larry and his family move into Prince's second home on Galpin Boulevard, just a stone's throw away from his main house on the same street.

One of the great things about being around Prince was that even though he was a genius, and wise beyond his years, he was also humble enough to be the student when he needed to be. This was the case with everyone he was around, whether he was talking to me, one of his attorneys, or a member of the cleaning crew, who scrubbed the toilets at Paisley. And it was certainly true with Larry. I don't say this lightly, but Prince idolized Larry. He saw something special in him that he wanted to learn from, and emulate! And, he soaked up everything he could.

Larry and Prince talked about everything, from playing the bass and navigating the music industry, to marriage and family. Because Larry was a devout Jehovah's Witness, the conversation would naturally flow to the Bible and God; the fact that Larry knew so much about God made Prince want to learn more, too. Prince started carrying his Bible with him everywhere he went, occasionally stopping to preach to anyone willing to listen. Eventually, Prince even started going door-to-door and evangelizing with Larry. I can't imagine the shock people must have had when they opened their door on a Saturday morning and saw Prince standing on their front stoop, ready to share the gospel!!! But, that's just how it happened! When Prince decided to do something, he went all-in. And becoming a Jehovah's Witness proved to be no different.

Once Prince stopped cussing, that meant we stopped cussing, too! There wasn't a formal rule or anything, but as with anything else, we all knew to just follow the boss' lead. If somebody got caught slipping, he'd call out, "Where's the swear jar!" Prince started making the women he was seeing change religion and become a Jehovah's Witnesses. He even tried to declare that anyone working for him would have to convert or get fired immediately. I think a couple people did convert, but he knew I wasn't going for it. I was crystal clear that I had already declared Jesus Christ as my Lord and Savior and that was that. However, despite my own religious convictions, I did go to the Kingdom Hall with Prince from time to time. Prince was comfortable being alone. He didn't have many real friends, so when he wanted someone to go and worship with him, a few of us rolled out with him to keep him company. He was my brother after all, and because of my love for him, I was willing to support him in his spiritual growth.

Everything was going well until, at some point, Prince felt that his growth had been stifled by the very organization that he had turned to for guidance.

To be clear, Prince had always believed in God. The notion that he was some kind of devil worshipper was completely false! And, to be honest, hilarious!

Yes. Prince was a sexual being! And, yes! He pushed the envelope beyond what other artists would even consider; daring to reveal the inner freak that he believed lives in all of us. But, that never meant he didn't love God!

Prince and I sat in the Paisley salon many nights, reading the tabloids, and cracking up over the ridiculous headlines that declared him a demon doing the work of Satan. Our running joke was, "Whatever people don't know, they'll just make up."

The truth is that Prince couldn't have made it that far without faith. It was always there, and it only grew stronger over time. When he met Larry, he wasn't coming from a place of atheism, or agnosticism. The seed had already been planted. Meanwhile, Prince was Prince. So, he took that little seed, watered it with Larry's teachings, and took it to the next level. Soon, Prince had outstudied and out-researched the ministers on the roster. Once he felt they could no longer teach him anything new, Prince went to the highest person in the Jehovah's Witness organization, the person who was the equivalent of the Pope in the Catholic faith. He had a sit-down conversation with that man and asked all the questions he'd been collecting in his mind, and on paper. And, when that man couldn't answer all of his questions, and couldn't give him definitive responses on matters of the Spirit, something inside of Prince broke.

Here's what I know: You can't go to a man to get answers about God. You have to go to God yourself. That relationship has to be so strong! So secure, that you know, that you know, that you know, He's real! And it doesn't matter what any one person says, or doesn't say. But Prince didn't know. He wasn't sure; he was still searching. And when he discovered that the Jehovah's Witnesses couldn't give him the answers he was searching for, he went out and tried to find them himself. He kept reading and studying, walking around with a duffel bag full of books, some holy, some not. The King James Bible, and the Witnesses Watchtower Bible were in there. There were also books on Hinduism, Buddhism, and every other religion known to man.

One night, I asked him, point-blank, "What is it that you're looking for?"

Paisley Park was Prince's creative battleship, and during the day, it was always hopping. The engineers were engineering, the musicians were making music, movies were being filmed, and videos were being edited. But at night, everybody left and went home to their families. So Prince would be alone, with the music, and with God; because God talked to him through the music. The night I asked him what he was searching for, I had stayed to keep him company. We were walking the empty halls of Paisley by ourselves, past all of the oddly-shaped furniture that I regularly bumped into, thinking it was Prince hiding in the shadows trying to scare me!

It had been a little while since Prince had left the Jehovah's Witness organization. Even though he still studied the Word, and would even lead our impromptu Bible studies (saying, "We're having church right now, because where two or three are gathered in his name, there He is also."). I knew he still wasn't settled in his spirit.

"Tell me what you're looking for," I repeated.

He paused for a while before answering, like he wanted to choose his words carefully. "I just need to be sure. I need evidence."

But there is no tangible evidence of faith, not in the way Prince was looking for it. He wanted an audible voice to call out from heaven, or a mystical deity to swoop down on a billowing cloud. It hadn't happened like that for him, but he was no stranger to signs of God. Once, when I had invited my mom, daughter, and niece, Ashlee, to Paisley Park. We were out running errands, for Prince, when we got caught in a ferocious storm. The sky went completely black, for a full 20 minutes, as baseball-sized hail poured down on the car we were in. I kept thinking that the windows were going to shatter, harming my baby and my niece in the backseat! But then, as sudden as it came, the storm left, and the sky returned to its formerly clear, blue state. As I pulled back up to Paisley, still shaking with fear, Prince was standing in the doorway. Marveling at God's majesty he asked, "Did you see that, Kim!? Did you see that amazing act of God?"

I knew God for myself, because I had seen him perform miracle after miracle in my own life. I'd witnessed my father live for seven years after open-heart surgery, even though doctors said he'd only survive six more months. Years later, my mother had a similar testimony after being diagnosed with stage-4 renal kidney disease. She was told she only had two weeks to live but is still alive and defying the odds to this day. I also saw how God raised my brother up from full paralysis caused by Guillain-Barre syndrome, and later delivered my newborn daughter from every diagnosis imaginable, including brain damage and possible cancer. I have seen God's hand in action. So, I knew what He could do.

Prince knew, too—he had witnessed many of the miracles in my life—yet he still wasn't sure. Prince only knew the certainties of Hollywood and the entertainment industry, of yes-men and groupies, of people who catered to him daily and made him feel "godly." Whenever he was feeling manipulative, he would say, "Anyone can be bought, Kim," and he'd flaunt his cash, making them bow down.

But all the yeses from the world can't compare to the goodness of God, or to His enduring faithfulness. That night in Paisley, Prince had lost touch with the real Truth, and he couldn't see that God was always present. He had forgotten that all the opportunities he was able to provide for so many people, as well as his ability to play 27 instruments, and to be able to entertain people all around the world, were miracles! We often need to be reminded of these things. I instantly realized that God had chosen me to be in

"Think big thoughts. But relish small things."[15]

—Jackson Brown, Jr.

Prince's life, to be a part of his journey, so that I could remind him that night.

"Sometimes God is just as plain and simple as the nose on your face," I said.

Prince didn't seem too convinced, so I said nothing more about it. We just kept walking, with only the voices of the doves filling up the empty space around us. The singing and squawking never bothered me during the day, but at 2 a.m. it sounded like fingernails on a chalkboard. "Don't the birds get on your nerves?" I asked, turning to Prince.

For the first time, Prince stopped walking. "The doves are my angels, and they help me create music," he said. He sounded bothered, like he couldn't believe I would ask such a stupid question. But as soon as he said the word "angels," all the annoyance melted from his face, replaced by a deep knowing. In that moment at least, Prince's eyes were opened, and he could see that everything in his life, including the doves, was a fulfillment of the promises God had made when he was just a boy.

Endorphinmachine

Wild and Loose, Natural, Beach wavy hairstyles textured look is great for summer

CREATE THESE HAIRSTYLES WITH A BEACH CHIC
TEXURIZING SPRAY

BRAID CRIMPING

Hit with Gina Rivera iron to fill in and untwist

MICRO-BRAID

This adds attitude to spice up any soft look
This can be placed in a part or along the hairline

CARAT

A DIAMOND'S WEIGHT, MEASURED *in carats, reflects its overall size. Of all the other factors to consider, the size and weight are the easiest, and most obvious, ways to determine a diamond's value. In fact, a diamond's carat weight often amplifies its other positive qualities.*

When Prince wrote the word "slave" on his face, he did it with such artistic precision that it seemed to be a part of some master plan. Like he had planned to do it for months, or weeks. On the contrary, however; the act that was one of the most controversial of Prince's career was one of sudden defiance! And it happened in a public restroom.

It was 1992, and there was a meeting set in the Burbank offices of Warner Brothers. Prince had recently signed a new deal with the label, worth $100 million for ten albums. But, his unaddressed frustrations were beginning to bubble to the surface. Prince's deal was fair by industry standards. It was generous, even, considering the deals that other artists were getting. But there was one sticking point that Prince couldn't get past.

No matter how much money Prince had made for Warner Brothers, and no matter how many millions of fans were waiting anxiously for his next project, the label still controlled how and when Prince could release new music.

Prince often said, "Record companies are great for some artists, but not this one."

After all, he was a self-contained musical genius who wrote, composed, and produced all of his music in his own luxury studio that contained the best, state-of-the art equipment that money could buy. He had all the capabilities to do what any label could do, and he knew he could do it better. He also recorded enough music to release a new album almost every day, but he couldn't do so without Warner Brothers approval. They had the final say because they owned the masters to all of his recordings, and with the masters comes the power!

Prince signed his first deal with Warner Brothers when he was still a teenager. In that deal, he was able to secure full creative control over his first three albums, as well as the rights to his own publishing. But as he admitted many years later, there was so much he didn't know about the music industry at that time. It took 14 years from the release of his first album for Prince to learn that he would be, to the music industry, what Harriet Tubman was to slavery. And that there was only one way for artists to protect and control their creative legacies: They must own their masters.

Even though his contract stated otherwise, Prince was adamant that he should have the final say over his intellectual property and how it was distributed. His argument: How could someone who was not in the studio, and who had no involvement in his creative output (which was downloaded directly from God), reduce his value and restrict his movement within the industry? In Prince's mind, it was commercial control and it was completely unfair. In fact, it was this realization that encouraged him to empower his team so that we could be effective agents of change in our own communities, even outside of music.

When Prince and I went into business together, he gave me his black AMEX card and told me to go create a space that would make money for myself, and my family, for years to come. Naturally, I opened a salon. I called it *The First Lady Salon & Spa*, primarily because most of my clients were the first ladies of L.A.-area churches, but also because I wanted every woman to know that when she stepped into the salon, she would receive the same star experience as a first lady, regardless of her background.

The salon sat on a huge shopping center lot at the corner of South La Brea Avenue and Rodeo Road in Los Angeles. The front of the salon faced "The Jungle", which most would categorize as one of L.A.'s worst neighborhoods, while the back of the salon sat on the cusp of Baldwin Hills, where many of the city's affluent African Americans live. Putting the salon in that location was an attempt to bridge the two communities, proving that they had more in common than not. Lavel DeLone, my daughter Sieara's father, designed the salon, and with over 2,000 square feet of opulence, from marble floors to a uniquely themed visual experience in each room, I often said that we had brought Beverly Hills to the hood.

> "*I had crossed the line. I was free;*
> *but, there was no one to welcome me*
> *to the land of freedom.*
> *I was a stranger in a strange land.*"[16]
> —Harriet Tubman

We offered various community services, including HIV testing, breast cancer screening, toy and clothing drives, and a welfare-to-work program sponsored by the organization My Girlfriend's Closet, which was run by Kimberly Ervin, First Lady of Church One in Long Beach. And, of course, we did hair.

Prince came to the salon to get his hair done just like everybody else, and the clients' excitement rose to another level when he showed up. They tried to act like they were unconcerned, but they couldn't help themselves. He often gave them an extra thrill by actually walking through the front door, even though he had his own "Bat-cave" entrance and a private lair where no one would ever see him. But that was Prince—always wanting to be normal. You could hear the women speaking through the walls: "He's right there! I saw him; he's right there!"

It was impossible for Prince to go unnoticed, and for the most part, he was accommodating to fans. Once, we were standing in front of the shopping center, not far from the salon, when an older woman, probably in her eighties, approached Prince. She narrowed her eyes and peered at him before saying, "Are you who I think you are?"

Prince smiled and said politely, "Yes, ma'am."

"Are you the young man that sings *Purple Rain*? Cause that's my favorite song."

"Yes ma'am," Prince repeated.

The lady nodded in approval, then she put her hands on both of his cheeks and whispered, "You just keep doing what you're doing, and God is going to bless your every step."

She slipped away, and for a moment, Prince and I were frozen in time, knowing that we had just spoken with an angel. We turned around to see where she had gone, but I couldn't see even a trace of her. What I did see, however, was the traffic on La Brea coming to a screeching halt as people began noticing Prince. One by one, cars stopped in the middle of the busy thoroughfare, the doors flew open, and people jumped out, screaming, "It's Prince! It's Prince!"

"Boss, we gotta go!" I said with my voice already tinged in fear.

But Prince was still in a trance, still mesmerized by the angel in our mist. "No, Kim," he said, softly. "It's fine."

I ignored him. There was no way I was going to let him get mobbed in the middle of L.A. with no security detail to be found. In an instant, I grabbed Prince's arm and dragged him back to the limousine like a lion carrying her cub in her jaws! I threw him in the back seat and instructed the driver to drive as fast as he could, before I turned and ran back to the salon.

The mob was close behind me, and by the time I reached the door, they were panting like rabid dogs, begging to see Prince. I played it off, and said I didn't know what they were talking about. It took some convincing, but they all sulked away eventually, disappointed that they had missed the chance to meet their idol in the flesh. Years later, Prince and I were still laughing about our adventure on La Brea.

The day of the Warner Brothers meeting, Prince walked into the conference room determined to make his point clear, and to have his requests honored. He was ready to make a deal, and he expected to be treated like the artist he was—a global superstar who had sold millions of records for the label. But Warner Brothers wasn't budging. Prince owned the rights to his publishing. Yes! But, Warner Brothers owned his master recordings, and that wasn't going to change. Prince could deliver, as much music as he wanted, but the label made the final determination on what, if anything, would happen with it.

In the face of firm opposition, Prince politely excused himself from the table, went to the men's bathroom, and used an eyeliner pencil to carefully pen the word SLAVE across his right cheek. He rewrote that word on his face day after day, for the next four years until he was released from Warner Brothers by a team of attorneys, led by the dynamic Londell McMillan. A man whom Prince nicknamed, the "Great Emancipator"! Once Prince was freed from his Warner Brothers deal, He was free to drop his 1996 album, aptly titled *Emancipation* via a joint partnership between his own NPG Records and EMI.

Looking back on this incident 25 years after it happened— and after multiple journalists, attorneys, and industry experts have attempted to analyze Prince's decision and its ramifications—it's easy to forget how truly groundbreaking it was. This was the early nineties, well before artists were regularly making public declarations about their personal or political views, or pitting themselves against major corporations. It kicked off a major shift in the way artists leveraged their power, but speaking out against an entity as large and as powerful as Warner Brothers was one thing. Evoking images of U.S. chattel slavery, in the process, was something else entirely.

Prince understood all that, and as he always did, he pressed forward under his own convictions. He was *Prince*! And he wasn't going to back down from what he believed to be blatant mistreatment. In tagging his face with one of the heaviest words in the English language, a word that carries such a dark and traumatic legacy, he was declaring all-out war on Warner Brothers. In many instances, he faced ridicule for it. Some of the same fans and media outlets that called him an icon after his death and remembered his fight against Warner Brothers as courageous, and revolutionary, had previously mocked him.

After the meeting, Prince met me at the Beverly Hills Hotel so I could do his hair. As soon as I saw him my mouth dropped open. "Why do you have 'slave' written on your face!?!" I said.

"Because I'm being enslaved." He shrugged. His face bore no expression other than the black letters etched onto his skin. "They own my masters, so they think they own me."

I must have been standing there speechless because, in an attempt to further explain himself, he added, "Kim, what's the opposite of 'master?'"

Leave it to the most creative artist in the world to devise an ingenious way to push back against his label. Unfortunately, Prince quickly learned that he wasn't going to be able to escape his contractual obligations with Warner Brothers, and he would still have to deliver the remaining albums in his deal. He felt trapped, but he wasn't going to give up. When we talked about the situation, I could see the wheels turning in his head. And he was committed to beating Warner Brothers at their own game.

About two months after the meeting, he had a plan:

First, he would pull music from his vault to close out his contract. He had rows and rows of music that hadn't been released, and while he didn't feel that all of it was his best work, he knew he didn't want to put any more energy toward the relationship with Warner Brothers. He had hundreds, if not thousands, of songs that he had never used. So, sending some of them over to the label, ever so methodically, would be the quickest and easiest way to get out of the deal. Prince knew how many projects he had to deliver, so when he was on a deadline, he would just casually reach into his catalogue and pull one out, the same way another man might choose which shirt he wanted to wear to work.

Second, if Warner Brothers were going to control what he did under the name Prince Rogers Nelson, the name that was given to him by his father, he would simply change it.

In a 1996 letter that was posted on his first website *thedawn.com*, excerpts from what Prince wrote:

"The first step I have taken towards the ultimate goal of emancipation from the chains that bind me to Warner Bros. is to change my name from Prince to O(+>). Prince is the name that my Mother gave me at birth. Warner Bros. took the name, trademarked it, and used it as the main marketing tool to promote all of the music that I wrote. The company owns the name Prince and all related music marketed under Prince. I became merely a pawn used to produce more money for Warner Bros.

By my 35th birthday, June 7, 1993, I was beyond frustrated with my lack of control over my career and music. It seemed reminiscent of much that had been experienced by other African-Americans over last couple of hundred years. They had turned me into a slave and I wanted no more of it. The dilemma had only one clear solution. I was born Prince and did not want to adopt another conventional name. The only acceptable replacement for my name, and my identity, was O(+>), a symbol with no pronunciation, that is a representation of me and what my music is about. This symbol is present in my work over the years; it is a concept that has evolved from my frustration; it is who I am. It is my name."[17]

Prince wasn't just another artist on the Warner Brother's roster. He knew his track record and his value, so he felt that his weight in the game should give him the opportunity to call his own shots. When it didn't, he poured all of his energy into the creation of his alter egos that could, in fact, remain independent. In addition to the Love Symbol, Prince adopted a moniker known as Tora Tora. Tora Tora was like a masked bandit, his face always covered with a veil or a scarf, and he represented Prince's desire to create and live anonymously, free from the concerns or expectations of others. Current artists like Sia and H.E.R. have adopted this desire to keep their appearances hidden so all focus is on their music, but the Purple One "hit it first."

The creation of alternate personalities was nothing new for Prince, of course. Since the beginning of his career, he had always used his talent to transform other artists and musicians into well-drawn characters—and then turn them into stars.

Prince met Morris Day when they were both in high school. Prince was living with Andre Anderson at the time (Andre changed his last name later to Cymone), and after hearing Morris play drums, Andre suggested that Morris join Prince and Andre's band, Grand Central. Even as kids they were booking gigs around Minneapolis, and Morris would later say that being around both Prince and Andre really showed him what it took to be a serious, professional musician.

After finding success as a solo artist, Prince went back to those early relationships and formed The Time. A band comprised of several of his former classmates, including producers Jimmy Jam and Terry Lewis, on keys and bass, respectively, and Morris as the lead singer. Along with Morris, Prince wrote and produced the entire album, which was recorded in Prince's studio outside of Minneapolis. Prince bragged about developing The Time, but it wasn't just the music that he was proud of. It was also the personalities that Prince created within the band that contributed to its success.

Prince knew his mother used to run from one relationship to the next, to feed her drug habit, never providing the nurturing love that he needed as a child (and as a man). As a result, he never displayed any real respect for any of the woman who came into his life after her. There was a rumor that he and Andre had gotten caught in Andre's basement, having an orgy. Prince didn't deny it, and his tendency to view women as objects designed solely for his sexual pleasure never waned. With Morris Day as the lead singer of The Time, Prince had an opportunity to create a character who embodied the animal-istic sexual desires warring within him. Morris wasn't just the charismatic leader with the fly dance moves. He was the slick hustler! The cat with the flashy car, and the diamonds to match! The one who had women tripping over themselves to take a turn in his bed! "Morris is the pimp side of me," Prince explained.

Later, I told Prince how I found out that three of my five brothers had different fathers. Will, my youngest brother, the one who loved to start some mess, had walked up to me one day and said, "You know they ain't your real brothers, right?" He didn't even wait for me to respond before adding, "Can't you see that they're light skinned and we're dark skinned?"

Before that, I had never paid attention to our skin color, but it was like a light bulb had suddenly been flipped. I ran to my mother, expecting a full explanation, but she just waved a dismissive hand. "We don't do steps, and we don't do halves. The same blood that flows through my veins flows through every one of yours. Those are your brothers."

Prince was laughing by the end of my story, after keying in on the fact that my mother had more than one baby daddy.

"Oh, so your mama was a rolling stone?" he said, trying to keep a straight face. "Cause mine was, too."

I know that Prince still harbored resentment toward his mother, even as an adult. It showed up in his sexual escapades and often in his music. But while Prince begging for a woman to let him "Take care of you and do all the things that only a best friend can," it was Morris who was dressed in head-to-toe leopard print, checking his image in a mirror mid-performance, and singing about having "ladies by the dozens" and "money by the tons."

Everyone in Prince's life became a character of his design, and people were happy to oblige if it meant they could spend even one more day with the Purple One. Prince even made a character of himself after going on tour with Rick James in 1979. Rick James's persona was built upon his freakiness, but Prince was determined to out-freak the Super Freak. He was sexual but mysterious, performing in full makeup, high-heeled boots, and skin-bearing costumes, even while referencing female love interests. Then, while wearing those high-heeled boots, he'd jump off speakers and slide down into the splits with a microphone between his legs. Prince embodied the funkiness of James Brown, the laid-back genius of Miles Davis, and the rollicking good time of Chuck Berry in one package. Nobody ever grooved harder than Prince on stage, and while Michael Jackson was a beast in his own right, Prince would often say, "Michael Jackson is the Disneyland version. If you want it raw and sexy, you rock with me."

> *"Without God*
> *It's just the blind*
> *Leading the blind"*[18]
>
> **—From the song**
> **"Colonized Mind"**
> **by Prince**

Prince's whole world, from his home, to the studio, to the stage was fashioned in his hypersexualized identity. When he traveled, his personal assistant and I had to go ahead of him, preparing his hotel room for his arrival. We were the "Foo Foo Girls," and it was our job to preserve Prince's sexy when he was on the road. We sounded like a small train pushing through hotel lobbies around the world with a dozen cases of Prince's favorite things, but we didn't have a choice. Everything had to be exactly as it was at home.

We carried lava lamps of all different sizes and colors, along with bushels of fabric in various shades of gold and red that we would drape over the hotel lamps and light fixtures to cast a sensual ambience around the room. We dropped the bed to the floor and covered it with goose down pillows so Prince would feel like he was sleeping on a cloud. And we brought his own personal rugs from Paisley, covering the floor with them so Prince's feet would never have to touch the ground. They were white, shaggy, and so plush your feet would disappear when you sunk your feet into them. Around the room were bowls filled with Prince's favorite treats: Tootsie Roll suckers, chocolate chip cookies, fruit, and herbal teas in every flavor. He had to have his favorite magazines, and they had to be untouched. If a magazine had already been read, or even opened, Prince would throw it to the ground and request a new one. His makeup and toiletries had to be arranged in the bathroom just so! The windows were completely blacked out.

We lit so much incense that the room smelled like Arabia awaiting its Prince.

There were no hoops that we wouldn't jump through to ensure that Prince's accommodations were perfect, and the most important accessory, the item that was a non-negotiable whether we were in Vegas or Venice, was a baby grand piano. I remember one hotel having to raise the piano on an outdoor lift and deliver it through the window because it wouldn't fit in the elevator! They were willing to do it because they wanted

Prince's business that badly. Meanwhile, Prince was just enjoying the perks of his fame.

Aside from using his money and power to help the members of his inner circle establish their own enduring legacies, Prince was most passionate about helping other artists. After he saw how the execs at Warner Brothers treated him, having little regard for his massive fame, he became determined to help other artists who were talented, but not yet established. His number one piece of advice: Don't sign a contract! Ever!

When D'Angelo visited Paisley Park he was already building a buzz in the industry by writing and producing songs for other artists, but he had yet to release his own breakout album *Brown Sugar*. D'Angelo was talented and soulful—just the kind of artist Prince liked to take under his wing. Prince showed him around Paisley before sitting him

"Freedom lies in being bold."[19]

—Robert Frost

down to have a long, in-depth conversation about the industry. Prince told him about his history in the music business and his current issues with Warner Brothers, openly sharing all the things he regretted, and the decisions he wished he could take back. He told him, "Man, you got *it*—that 'it' factor that's going to take you right to the top." He paused, but then added, "Just don't get in bed with these white folks."

Prince pointed out the wardroom room, the rehearsal room, and the room where he edited his films. Then, as he did with every artist who visited Paisley, from Erykah Badu to Chaka Khan, he took D'Angelo into the studio so they could vibe out, creating what I'm sure is some of the best music locked up in the vault. All of this was done to show D'Angelo that he had enough talent to secure his rung on the industry ladder without taking anything from the powers that be.

Unfortunately, Prince's advice was too little, too late. D'Angelo had already signed a publishing deal with EMI, and his debut album was forthcoming. *Brown Sugar* did well, and Prince was happy for the success of songs like "Lady," "Cruisin," and the title track, but he was disappointed that he hadn't gotten to him early enough.

Seeing how much he cared and how much he wanted to keep other artists from making the same mistakes he had, I asked him the same question I had been asking more and more frequently, especially after the Warner Brothers battle. "Why don't you just write a book and tell people how to make it in the music business?"

Like clockwork, his answer was the same as it had been every other time I'd asked. "If people want to learn, they need to watch what I'm doing, and they need to follow my lead."

At the time, I thought it was selfish that he wouldn't just lay out a blueprint so artists could know exactly what to do, and what not to do, as they made their way in the music business. But now, many years later, I think I understand. In Mark 4:12, Jesus explains why he teaches in parables, and contrary to popular belief, it wasn't with the intention of making his messages easier to understand. Jesus said that people will be "ever seeing but never perceiving" and "ever hearing but never understanding," which is to say that the Truth was there, but it was hidden. And while Jesus left it up to the general public to keep searching, to prove their desire for Knowledge, he gave it freely to His disciples who had already given up everything to follow Him. Likewise, for

"We are warriors who serve Good and Light in the Universe Sometimes we rescue; sometimes we guide"[20]

—**From the movie** *A Wrinkle in Time*

artists who were willing to listen and take Prince's advice, he dished it out in copious amounts. In every case they benefitted from Prince's tutelage, whether it was Nona Gaye regaining the rights to her father's masters, or George Clinton gaining a new label home, and the right to create innovative, genre-breaking music again.

Prince wanted to lead a global revolution of artists reclaiming control of their music. But, he only wanted to teach and guide those who were serious about their art. Who had perfected their craft and were at the top of their game. He knew it would take strong resolve, and skill, to overthrow the suits in the executive offices. So he was careful in choosing those whom he would personally lead. More often than not, those people were women.

Kim Berry

114

Endorphinmachine

COLOR ME BAD

Grey hair trends are not going away

CHARCOAL MILKSHAKE

BLACK PEARL

COPPER

SMOKEY PINK

(a grown up version of pink with sophisticated undertones)

CERTIFICATION

EVALUATING A DIAMOND *based on certain qualifications, including cut, color, clarity, and carat, is only one part of determining its true value. In fact, this evaluation should come from a reputable, third party organization that can objectively verify each of the diamond's characteristics, thus certifying its worth.*

Like I said, Prince was a master at spotting talent, and he had a way of finding people who were hidden in obscurity, molding them, and then gracing them with his stamp of approval before catapulting them to stardom. Many of Prince's interactions with women were often underscored by his general distrust and lack of respect for females. But when Prince connected with a woman through music—that is when she exhibited her own talent and creativity, and she could hold her own with him—those relationships were some of the most fulfilling for him. Music was Prince's spiritual release. So, finding someone who could meet him on that level was particularly rewarding. This was the type of connection that he had with Sheena Easton, Sheila E., Mayte Garcia, Tamar, Andy Allo, and many others. They were artists whose sound he helped to cultivate, whether he wrote one song for them or produced an entire album. But female musicians didn't have to sing in order to vibe with Prince. Well before Beyonce put together her first all-female band, Prince was bucking industry traditions and hiring women musicians, whether they played keys, bass, guitar, or drums.

Cora Dunham is a world-renowned drummer who has traveled the globe with Beyonce and other artists. In addition to serving as musical director for the Black Girls Rock Awards she became an author and philanthropist. She was just as talented when Prince, his personal assistant Ruth, and I met her on a late night in L.A. At the time, she was like most gigging musicians. Fresh out of Howard University, and picking up shows here and there.

Prince was feeling antsy that evening, so he asked me to come do his hair in case he wanted to go out. While I was hooking him up, he asked me if I knew of any jazz clubs around town. He wanted something small, so he could hang out without attracting a lot of attention. I finished up his hair and got on the phone to put some feelers out. As always, I had to be ready to deliver when Prince made a request, and deliver I did. I found a small club on Wilshire, where Frank McComb and his band were playing. Before we even walked in, Frank's smooth, soulful vocals floated out the front door and grabbed us by the heart. If I had closed my eyes and didn't know any better, I would've guessed Donny Hathaway had come back to grace us with one more set. After we walked in and found a seat, we quickly realized that Frank wasn't the only superstar on the stage.

Cora was on drums and commanding the groove, staying in the pocket but getting funky when she needed to. Prince, Ruth, and I were at a corner table off in the cut, and he couldn't take his eyes off of Cora. Finally, when the band took a break, Prince told me to ask Cora to come over to the table to talk to him. The introductions were smooth, and Cora took to meeting Prince like a pro. There was no geeking out, or obvious fan-girling (though I'm sure she probably was on the inside).

After some heavy conversation between sets, in perfect Prince fashion, he asked her about her dream drum set - the one she'd play if she had her pick of all the kits ever built. I saw the surprise and confusion creep across her face, but she told him her choice anyway. Immediately, Prince looked over at Ruth and said, "Order it!"

Prince was like Willy Wonka, and Cora had just scored her very own golden ticket! The time she spent with Prince over the following years, absorbing the creative energy that permeated Paisley Park, was surely some of the most transformative of her career. Cora's talent was undeniable (still is). And, in the same way he did for musicians like Lisa Coleman, Wendy Melvoin, Rhonda Smith, Kat Dyson, and Candy Dulfer, Prince's endorsement leveled up her game in extraordinary ways! Carrying her on to stages with a bevy of artists including Pink and Ledisi.

Prince was able to instill a degree of confidence and swagger in everyone he met, by simply being himself and exercising his innate ability to pull the best out of everyone. I know this, personally, because he did the same for me. I was the non-musical entity in his life, a hairstylist and confidante. He trusted me. He trusted my perspective when he shared his deepest fears and secrets, and he trusted my opinion—on the best jazz spots in L.A. as well as countless other topics that came up over the many years I worked with him. Prince even trusted me to contribute to the very thing that meant the most to him: his music. Sometimes, when he was recording late and Paisley was empty, except for me and the doves, Prince would tell me he needed another voice on a track he was working on. He'd call me into the studio and put me in the booth, auto-tuning me until he got just what he needed to execute his vision. There was nothing that was going to stop him from creating, and he knew how to make even me, his hairstylist, sound good.

We can't forget that when it came down to it, most of the women in Prince's life were there for a primary purpose that had very little to do with music. (With that said, we also know that few of the women who claimed to have slept with Prince actually did—a fact that was proven by the barrage of people who jumped on the would-be gravy train to DNA-Nowheresville after his death.)

When Ludacris wrote the song "Area Codes" and rapped about having women all over the world, he must have been inspired by Prince. He *had* to, because that man had so many females it was impossible for me to keep up with them all. Whether he was on tour, or traveling on vacation, there were always beautiful women waiting on him at the airport, or hotel. And, no matter who they were, or where they were from, the story was always the same in each of their minds. "She was *dating* Prince!" "She was the only woman in his life"; and "she" would be the one to get him to settle down and put a ring on it! But, they had no idea, that for the vast majority of his life, Prince's only true love was his music. Everyone else was his mistress.

Like he did with Morris Day of The Time, Prince created an image, or character, for each of his female playthings. Molding them into a version of themselves that even they weren't familiar with. They went along with it, of course! And, every bit of personal care, and attention, they received from Prince made them believe that he loved them more than all the others. In reality, though, they were just the flavor of the moment. The newest doll he could dress up and, later, undress. The neighborhood baller might take you out to dinner, and buy you some new shoes, but Prince's game was on a completely different level. He would fly women around the world, shoot videos and movies about them, send them on shopping sprees, produce albums for them, and even send them out on tour!

He absolutely did these things, but he never implied any true commitment on his part. Prince was the master of his Monopoly board, moving pieces in, out, and all around according to his feelings on any given day.

I called most of these women fly-by-nights. Prince had me do their hair, whether they were in his life for three minutes or three years, and as soon as they got in my chair, they were so excited, their voices high-pitched, and anxious as they introduced themselves. I politely ignored them, each time, hearing Craig Mack's voice in my head. "You won't be around next year!" Sure enough, by the time I returned to Paisley they were always gone. Replaced by the next fly-by-nighter. No matter how many females had come before, each new woman Prince was entertaining thought she was more special, more beautiful than all the others. They all thought they were different! That they had what it took to stick around long-term. And for some strange reason, they all thought I would give them the inside secrets on how to do it!

"Prince is such a great guy, and I want him to love me," they'd say. "What do I need to do? Or say? Or not do? Or not say?" I would just stand there, curling their hair, smiling but refusing to respond. My check was signed by Prince Rogers Nelson, there was no way I was giving up any information to a woman who'd probably only be around for a month or two, if that!

It's important to note that these women weren't famous when Prince met them. He preferred his women unknown, without a past, and without any celebrity exes. He reveled in the knowledge that he put them on the map! They were lost in oblivion until the paparazzi snapped the perfect shot of them with Prince, or they landed in a video or on their own tour. All of the women were just toys to play with, so to speak. And, when he was done with them, he gave them a parting gift and sent them on their way.

I was trained in the Prince methods early on, so nothing ever shocked me. Over time I got used to the constant trail of women that came in and out of Paisley. And now, well after the fact, his list of conquests reads like a Hollywood who's who! Vanessa Marcil, Mel B, Chili, Rosario Dawson, Ananda Lewis… It just goes on and on.

Prince definitely had a type. He liked his women petite, and after he broke things off with Vanity (his first true love), most of the women he dated, as well as both of the women he married, had a similar look. I liked to say they were "Vanity-esque". There were some exceptions, however, including a couple of dark-skinned beauties. There was also a young white woman named Tara Leigh Patrick, whom Prince eventually turned into Carmen Electra. Carmen was a budding artist he met at a show. And, while he groomed her, and helped her with her music, their relationship also became sexual.

> *"Until the end of time, I'll B There 4 U*
> *U own my heart N mind*
> *Eye truly adore U"[21]*
> **—From the song "Adore" by Prince**

Prince was still dating Carmen Electra when he met Mayte Garcia, a teen-aged belly dancer. Women were in and out of Prince's life like cars at a mechanic's garage. But, there was something different about Mayte. They clicked! And even before their relationship grew intimate, Prince began prepping Carmen for her own tour—a clear signal that the tide was changing. Prince might juggle two, three, or more women at a time, but we all knew that the woman inside Paisley was the only woman who really mattered.

Mayte's dad was in the military, so her family essentially

traveled for a living. This made it easy to follow Prince around on tour, and Mayte's mom, Nelle, had no problem with that. So, from the very beginning she was the mastermind of their relationship, and was determined to insert her daughter into Prince's life.

Nelle and Mayte first started showing up at U.S. concerts, with Nelle waiting at the back door of the venue after a show, trying to catch someone from Prince's camp. After a while we began to expect it, to know that she'd be outside after every concert, but I think we were all surprised when she started showing up at the international shows. It was then that I finally understood the extent of Nelle's hustle.

I was constantly running back and forth to the bus, always granting whatever wish Prince currently desired. After lurking in the shadows night after night, Nelle finally got my attention, and she shoved a VHS tape of Mayte's performances into my hands. I reluctantly accepted it and went to take it to Prince, but I couldn't even get close to him before he started rolling his eyes, giving me my cue to toss it in the trash. The next time Nelle appeared, the tape was passed to Kirk, one of the dancers. Kirk was more successful than I had been, and he actually got Prince to watch it. The tape showed Mayte from age two to 16, bellydancing all over the world. As soon as the tape ended, Prince told Kirk, "Bring her back here."

I was taken aback by his request. Nelle had come off as very aggressive, almost like she was pimping her daughter. But Prince had made up his mind, so that was that. As directed, Mayte was brought backstage, and she met Prince in his dressing room. Once she was settled in, Prince started her tape over and they watched it together, laughing and making jokes with each other like old friends. The chemistry was there even then—not in a romantic way, but more like a spiritual connection, as if they'd known each other for years.

Since they'd hit it off so well, and Prince was definitely intrigued by Mayte's artistry. He invited her back to Minnesota after the tour was over. She visited Paisley and hung out with Prince even more, and it wasn't long before she became an official member of NPG. Like all of the other women he worked with, Mayte needed a persona, and because Prince was fascinated with Egypt at the time, he decided that Mayte's character would be that of an Egyptian Princess. Mayte was actually from Puerto Rico, but that never stopped Prince from telling the story, and it never stopped Mayte from going along with it. Mayte's charm and talent had Prince completely engrossed, so much so, that they started spending even more time together outside of rehearsals and shows. Eventually, Prince discovered that Nelle had lied to him. Mayte wasn't an 18-year-old high school graduate, as he'd been told. She was only 16! And she was being homeschooled as her family traveled from city to city.

Once the truth about Mayte's age finally came out, a bigger problem was realized. Mayte was still a minor, and living on her own, without guardianship, which was illegal. Because Prince had already set Mayte up in her own place, it would have been very easy for him to call Nelle and fly her up to Chanhassen to move in with Mayte. But Prince didn't allow the people around him to have entourages—even if those entourages consisted of their own family members. In Prince's mind, the only solution was for him to become Mayte's legal guardian. Surprisingly (or not, considering how hard she'd worked to get Mayte's tape to Prince), Nelle willingly signed away her parental rights. I can't even imagine giving my daughter over to some man I didn't know! But, for Nelle, letting Mayte stay with Prince must have been the manifestation of everything she had hoped for! The happy ending, after countless hours in planes and cars! So she could snag the attention of the most talented man in the world.

Even after the ink on the custody agreement had dried, Mayte's dancing career didn't take off as quickly as she probably assumed it would. She had to spend a while in the background before she got her chance to shine. She was supposed to be in the "Diamonds and Pearls" video, but Diamond, the other dancer, refused to share the screen with Mayte. She must have instinctively known that Mayte was being groomed to be her replacement, and she was trying to fight off the inevitable for as long as possible. But Prince was continuing to spin the tale of Mayte as an Egyptian Princess. And she ultimately became the muse for his 1992 album *Love Symbol*. To promote the album, Prince created a direct-to-video film by compiling videos of some of the songs and tying them together with the "3 Chains O' Gold" plotline. The premise of the story was that seven men had murdered the father of an Egyptian Princess (played by Mayte), in an effort to get their hands on the 3 Chains of Gold. Mayte was forced to join forces with Prince in order to protect the treasure, and along the way, they fell in love. Prince even hired renowned film director, Randee St. Nicholas, to shoot a video with Mayte in the deserts of Egypt.

Back at Paisley, the real Prince and Mayte weren't in love just yet. But they were definitely growing closer.

Mayte was very personable and easy to talk to, and she often told me, and some the rest of the crew, about her conversations with Prince. They often hypnotized each other, she said, as this was their way of communicating freely, and when Prince was under hypnosis, he was more willing to speak about all of the women he'd been with. Because she knew he was under hypnosis, Mayte let it all slide, promising not to hold his indiscretions against him. When Mayte was under hypnosis, she talked about her past loves, too, and Prince granted her the same protection from judgement. They believed they'd met previously in a past life and that they had been divinely brought back together in the present.

I don't know that Prince hypnotized all of his women, but when Mayte first mentioned it, I wasn't surprised at all. Prince was brilliant, always talking about space, time travel, quantum physics, and similar concepts. He'd say things like, "Kim, if you want to be in Hawaii, you just have to imagine yourself in Hawaii, and you'll be there. You can feel the sand and the water now; just feel it in your mind." Prince always had next-level thinking, and the idea that our minds can take us wherever we want to go was the premise behind the lyric, "*Meet me in another world, space and joy*," from the song "Girls & Boys."[22]

Not every woman could get with this out-the-box mindset. So, I knew that once he started sharing these thoughts and ideas with Mayte—and she went along with them without thinking he was strange—she was going to be around for a while. She was also accepting of his wild, bachelor lifestyle, even if that acceptance was induced by hypnotism. In fact, when they got married years later, Prince wrote in the wedding program that Mayte had stolen his heart because she was the most under-standing of all the women he'd ever been with. I don't know if she understood Prince as much as she just accepted him for who he was, and as he was. Mayte ignored the other women, and she dutifully stayed at home, waiting on his calls while he was away. Prince was a lot to deal with, and Mayte figured out how to take it all in stride.

Once, when Mayte was in glam before a show, someone brought in a plate of food and set it next to her on the table filled with makeup brushes and hairspray. Prince came in the room, looked at the food in disgust, and said to Mayte bluntly, "Is that your plate?" He had previously accused Mayte of eating too much, so even though she told him the food belonged to one of the makeup artists, he immediately docked her pay for the week. Mayte was furious when she found out. Now, Mayte had been injured and wasn't able to dance as much as she had been before, so she might have actually picked up a couple pounds. She was still tiny, but, apparently, she wasn't tiny enough for Prince. Actually, Prince and Mayte were almost the exact same size and height. Sometimes she'd go shopping and buy a new pantsuit or a turtleneck, and before she'd even have a chance to step into them, Prince would carry them right up to the wardrobe room to have them tailored for his frame.

In retrospect, it's hard to pinpoint the exact moment that Prince and Mayte became a couple. They'd been hanging for a while, going to dinners and dragging the rest of us to the movies when Prince had rented out the whole theater. They never declared when they were official, but during rehearsals for a show, Prince's reaction to an incident made it very clear that Mayte was, indeed, his woman.

All the members of the New Power Generation got paid a base rate for each show, and they also got a bonus predicated on the excitement level of their performance. Prince encouraged everyone to do stunts—from the musicians to the dancers—and the crazier and funkier the stunts were, the better. Crewmembers got an extra $1,000-$5,000 depending on how wild they got. Mayte's thing was crowd surfing. It's commonplace now, and done at concerts large and small, but the first time Mayte did it, the fans had no clue. As soon as Mayte jumped out from the stage that first time, arms and legs splayed like she was floating in an Olympic-sized swimming pool, she fell right onto the ground. After a couple shows, the crowds started getting the hang of her routine, and they'd hold their arms out, begging Mayte to jump. Then they'd catch her and pass her around to the rest of the screaming fans.

The crowd surfing was cool, but it wasn't enough for Prince. In his mind, you could always get funkier, crazier, *and wilder*.

"Wouldn't it be cool if somebody shaved their head during the show?" Prince said during rehearsal one day. Prince was always over-the-top, so no one seemed to take this particular suggestion too seriously—no one but musical director Morris Hayes, that is. During the next show, right on cue, Morris stepped out from behind his keyboard, clippers in hand, and shaved his head in front of thousands of screaming fans.

Tommy Barbarella, not to be outdone, liked to swing from the rafters above the stage. It was a cool bit, him flying around with his keytar around his neck, but in an effort to prove that he was the craziest of them all, he took things a little too far during a rehearsal. Tommy was playing his keytar and prancing around the stage when, suddenly, he took the instrument and stuck it in between Mayte's legs. Let me tell you, it was just like someone had dragged a needle across a record. The music stopped *immediately*! Prince didn't have to say anything. The look on his face was enough to make it perfectly clear that Mayte was his, and no one else was to lay a hand on her. Mayte maintained the look of innocence that Prince had come to love, while Tommy backed away sheepishly. And, of course, he never went near Mayte again.

Tommy's mistake was relatively minor, but I still shook my head. At that point, I had been telling folks for a while: Don't go near Prince's women. Stay clear; don't be friendly; and don't hold too much conversation. It wasn't just about not upsetting Prince in the short term; eventually, when Prince dismissed his women (and they all, eventually, got dismissed) anyone who was close to them got dismissed too. I saw it all the time. Prince would send a girl packing, and every single member of the crew who was considered a friend of hers, from the makeup artists to the background singers, had to go. It was Prince's way of ensuring that once a woman was gone, she was really gone, because he wasn't interested in reliving the past. When he closed a chapter, he slammed the whole book shut and threw it into a blazing inferno!

For the time being, though, Mayte was the queen of Prince's chessboard, and his world revolved around her. Their relationship progressed like any normal relationship does— they spent more time together, had more talks, grew even closer. Consorting with Prince wasn't like dating a normal guy, of course, but their relationship was as normal as it could be within the confines of this rock star's Purple Universe. There were other women, as well as Prince's various demands and diva behavior, but Mayte adjusted her crown while establishing her stronghold in the kingdom. If Prince had other women in town, Mayte only came to Paisley after they had left for the day. By that time, Chanhassen was no longer the sleepy, middle-of-nowhere town that it was when Prince first moved there, so there were apartment buildings, grocery stores, restaurants, and, most importantly, hotels for Prince's *hot thangs*.

So how did we know things were *really* serious between him and Mayte? Well, I found out during a visit to the wardrobe department. No one, including Prince, ever explicitly stated that he and Mayte were getting married. But when I saw the dress that Bonnie, another member of the glam squad, was creating for Mayte, there was no question that it was a wedding gown! At the same time, Debbie and Prince were designing his wedding ensemble. It was nothing short of amazing! Nothing had slowed down at Paisley. There were still tours to plan for, rehearsals to make, and studio sessions to record. But somehow, in the midst of all of that, Mayte and Prince were planning a wedding.

Prince was the ultimate overseer, so you better believe he was hands-on with wedding planning, from day one. His first idea was to ship everyone over to Paris and do the ceremony big-baller style, but there wasn't time for that. Mayte and Prince started planning over the summer, and with the wedding date firmly set for Valentine's Day they had to bring in a wedding planner to ensure that everything was executed on schedule. But he was still very involved. He knew the flowers he wanted; he knew the music that would play during the ceremony; he knew that he wanted to have a casting call for the seven flower girls who preceded Mayte down the aisle. Prince wanted his wedding to be rocked-out from the top-out! In true superstar fashion! If you ask me, he was directing the greatest music video of his career.

Prince and Mayte settled on a small wedding in a Minneapolis church and a private dinner at Paisley Park, followed by a huge party at the soundstage for 1000 friends, staffers, and devoted fans.

The day of the ceremony, I showed up early in the morning

to do Prince's hair. He smelled like he'd bathed in a field of jasmine. His wedding garb, emblazoned with his love symbol fused with the letter M, was draped across the bed. As soon as he opened the door I could feel his joyous energy. "This is it! My wedding day!" he said, bowing. Then he started skipping around the room, giddy like a kid hyped up on too much candy. It was cute to see him so happy.

Once I finished styling Prince's hair, I had to get to the church to hook up the bride-to-be. There were paparazzi everywhere, including helicopters flying above, with everyone trying to get the perfect shot of the couple. Once inside, I rushed to join Donna Gregory, who was on makeup, and Bonnie, who was perfecting Mayte's gown. We were her Cinderella glam squad! By the time we were finished Mayte looked like an earth angel. I remember stepping back to look at her and being amazed at how much she'd matured. How her innocence had morphed into smoldering flames right before our eyes. She had gone from friend, to dancer, to lover, and wife. And, she had done it so gracefully. So effortlessly.

Because Prince wanted to keep the details of his wedding completely hidden, there were tents covering everything from the street, to the sidewalk, to the entire back of the church. He'd asked for a police escort to the church, planning to be delivered to the back door, so he could swoop in through the chaos at the last possible moment. The news had caught wind of his plan. So, in true Prince fashion, he got in the back of the van carrying the flowers and made it inside the venue undetected. Just like the nights he'd arrive at his concerts, chilling inside a black box that security rolled right up the stage! No one knew that he was right there, in their midst! And, ready to wed the most beautiful girl in the world.

Thousands of lilies, orchids, gardenias, and roses covered the sanctuary. It was a total surprise to everyone involved in the planning. Mayte had only ordered a few, but Prince, of course, wanted to go over the top. There would be no short-comings for his bride! Yet, for all the flowers in the room, there were very few guests. It was by design. During his interview with Oprah, at Paisley, Prince told her that he wanted to leave space for all of the angels who had descended from heaven to attend their nuptials. The program Prince created explored important details about his relationship with Mayte. Including the fact that July 25th was the date when he met her, and the date when he proposed, and that both of their fathers were named John! While musing whether their connection was coincidence or fate. But the most carefully crafted element of the entire ceremony was definitely the music. Prince wrote the album *Kamasutra* specifically for the wedding and specifically for Mayte.

The stage was set! The wedding party entered one by one, while I, along with Donna Gregory, and a chosen few of Prince's inner circle, filled just two of the church's pews. As the flower girls silently dropped their petals, a wave of sensual melodies rushed from the speakers to coincide with Mayte's entrance.

She was ethereal and gorgeous! Prince's perfect companion! As they stood next to each other, whispered their vows, and kissed, they officially became man and wife!

Endorphinmachine

PERFECTLY IMPERFECT DU'Z

BUN/TOPNOT

Tie your hair into a pony and before twisting into a bun
leave the ends loose and messy

THE BLOW DRY IS BACK!

Where there was an undone look, we will see a sleeker
smoother more polished look
This could be wavy, curly or straight

MESSY SEXY LOOK

Use a large iron to wand in the waves leaving the ends loose
to get that textured look
Naturally loose curls to achieve a Messy Sexy Look

TWIST OUT

Use your favorite curl pudding and stretch method
Allow hair to air dry
Use your favorite oil to add sheen to the twist out
for the finished look

THE MOST BEAUTIFUL GIRL IN THE WORLD

B EING MARRIED DIDN'T slow Prince down a bit. Which meant that Mayte couldn't slow down either. Prince said Mayte was his Muse, and that she was as much a part of the band as anyone else. Her body was her instrument. When she danced, he would stare at her so intensely you could feel the energy radiating from their bodies, almost like they were making love to each other in their minds.

Because I styled Mayte's hair, we had a lot of chances to talk and hang out. Our relationship was cool and easy. We chatted like home girls when she was in the chair! Unlike Prince's other women, she never asked me about Prince, never tried to get any scoop. They were so in tune with each other - their connection so deep - that she didn't feel the need to try to check up on him. But Prince was still Prince! And trust and believe, he flexed his clout whenever he got ready. In his eyes, Mayte belonged to him, and he made the rules. Between the shows and the constant rehearsals, Mayte danced for hours and hours each day. On top of that, Prince kept her on an eating regimen so strict, that she had to sneak to eat food; especially, if she wanted to eat meat! This went on after they got married and even during both of her pregnancies. Sadly, Prince was so devastated by the death of baby Amir that he needed someone to blame. And Mayte, who had continued to eat fish despite Prince's firm guidelines, and vegetarian diet, was an easy target.

Like the wedding, neither Prince nor Mayte spoke openly about the first pregnancy, or the miscarriage that followed. She'd lost the baby so early, that none of us had even noticed the change in her body. We only found out when she accidently let it slip during a wardrobe fitting. The second pregnancy, however, was completely different. We all knew that Mayte was carrying Prince's baby. Even though we were forbidden from talking about it to anyone on the outside, we loved on her extra hard! Then, when the tragedy struck, we tried to help both of them through it the best way we knew how.

Mayte was still touring with Prince, and the NPG, when she started getting sick. She was still dancing and training on a daily basis. Pushing her little body to the limits. But, we still felt blindsided when she started bleeding and experiencing intense pain. Just a few months into the pregnancy, it seemed as if her body was trying to abort the baby.

Mayte was placed on complete bed rest. And, even though the rest of us stayed out on tour, we went back to Minneapolis every couple days to visit her in the hospital. Prince flew in the best doctors from around the world to take care of her. They were doing everything they could to keep that baby in the oven as long as possible; including performing a Cerclage procedure to keep Mayte's cervix closed! Since she wasn't allowed to go back to Paisley, we had to keep her as comfortable as possible in the hospital. And that meant she had to stay glammed. There was no worry of reporters, or cameramen, showing up to the hospital to try to snap a picture, but Prince wanted her to be beautiful at all times. Her bed was configured so that we could push it directly into the shower. And, every other day I would visit, to shampoo, blow dry, and curl her hair.

The on-call beauty services were primarily Prince's wish, which I was happy to oblige. But one thing I wasn't going to do was keep Mayte's mother away from her.

It was ironic how it happened, that Prince and Nelle came to hate each other so much. As the saying goes, you gotta be careful what you wish for. Nelle had exerted every bit of her power to insert Mayte into Prince's life. But, when Mayte needed her mother most, Prince was exerting his power to keep Nelle out! Nelle had signed custody of Mayte over to Prince. But, after a while, she grew tired of his rules and his insistence on telling Mayte what to do. Mayte was pregnant! Why couldn't she enjoy herself and have a slice of cake if she wanted it? Nelle hated Prince! And, Prince could not have cared less! His perspective was: Mayte is my wife. And this is my family. Nobody is going to tell me what to do! In fact, I'm going to tell *you* what to do! And you can take your ass back home if you don't like it!

I loved and respected Prince, but his demands during Mayte's pregnancy were outrageous. So despite the fact that he was my boss, I, along with the hospital staff, snuck Nelle in and out each day, against Prince's wishes. I didn't think twice about it. There was no second-guessing.

"How could Eye 4get that U

R the RULE
U R my God
I am your child"[23]

—From the song
"Anna Stesia" by Prince

I knew that I would one day have my own child, and that I would want my mom by my side when I did. I also thought about my mom, and how she would have felt, if I were in Mayte's position. There was no way I could have dropped a dime and turned Nelle away.

The doctors and nurses set Nelle up in a room right next to Mayte's. She ducked in there each time we got word from security that Prince was on his way. We were discreet, but Prince had to have known that Nelle was still visiting her. He always called before he left Paisley to let us know he was on his way. And, without fail, he always asked, "Is she there, Kim?"

I lied every time.

Away from the hospital, I listened to Prince tell me why he felt the way he did about Mayte and Nelle, and about how he wanted things ran. Then, when I got back to the hospital, Nelle would cry and curse at Prince for treating her, and her daughter, so badly. I was in the middle, and it got uncomfortable at times, but I can't imagine what Mayte was going through. She loved her mother, and she loved her husband, but they were at each other's throats.

I worried about Prince, too. Each time he made a fuss about one trivial thing or another, my heart broke all over again for the pain I knew he still carried from his mother. In his eyes, his own mother had failed as a parent. As a result, I think he decided that women couldn't be trusted to raise emotionally stable children. He was adamant that every single decision made on behalf of his son would be made by him, and him alone! From the back-and-forth between Nelle and Mayte, to the Paisley craziness that never died down, I felt like I was watching an episode of the *Young and the Restless*; my mother's favorite soap opera, except I was actually a character in the plot!

Incidentally, my own personal life was non-existent. I was staying with Prince for stretches of six to eight months at a time and sending money back home to make sure my family was taken care of. There were no boyfriends. There weren't even any dates! For everyone in Prince's crew, his life became your life, and that was definitely the case for me. The crewmembers that had managed to maintain long-term relationships were only able to do so because they're significant others worked for Prince, too. Ultimately, all of us became family. We looked out for one another. Lifting each other's spirits when days got tough. We were all we had, really, because even if we did enter into a relationship with someone on the outside, it wouldn't last. How could we discuss the surreal experience of working with Prince to people who had no clue? How could we expect someone who worked a regular 9-5 job to understand that when we got a call to be at the airport in an hour, for an international tour, that we had to be there!? Working for one of the greatest entertainers in the world may have been a fairytale for others, but it was an everyday reality for us. In light of those truths, and maybe despite them, I didn't mind that I was single. I was young and able to travel the world with zero responsibilities! I was fully aware of how blessed I was! I never once felt like I was missing out on anything in those early years with Prince. It was simply our way of life! One that I grew accustomed to, especially as we neared a time when he would need me more than ever.

The closer we got to the baby's birth, the more excited we all were. Especially Prince! He had a nursery built, and beautifully decorated inside Paisley; he even had a swing set installed outside. Prince was ready to become a dad! And parenthood was affecting every part of him! He was becoming softer and more tolerant. A little less likely to cuss someone out! Then, a couple of months before the birth, we went to L.A. to tape an episode of *Muppets Tonight*. Prince was the special guest on the show, and it was truly amazing to see how he interacted with the Muppets! He was actually having *fun*.

"When something on the inside of you connects with what's happening outside of you,

it's a sign that a portion of your life is a part of the solution."[24]

—Sarah Jakes Roberts

Unfortunately, though, it didn't last.

Celebrity mom, Mayte, checked into the hospital under

the name, Mia Gregory, in order to avoid the paparazzi. While the name tag on the incubator read Boy Gregory, Prince and Mayte's son was born, Amir Nelson, on October 16,1996.

From the moment Amir appeared in the world, it was obvious that something wasn't right. He didn't cry, and his appearance was abnormal. The diagnosis wasn't immediate, but doctors soon discovered that Amir had been born with Pfeiffer Syndrome, a rare condition that causes certain bones of the skull to fuse together too soon, before the skull is finished developing. The shape of the head and face are affected, and people who have the condition often have protruding eyes, along with many other deformities. Baby Amir was going to have a long road ahead of him.

Prince later told me that Amir didn't make a sound when he was born and that he had to be rushed to the corner of the hospital room to be revived. Prince was devastated that what had started as a labor of love, and him believing God for a healthy child, had ended this way, and left Mayte a nervous wreck! The room quickly devolved into chaos, and disorder, until everyone in the room finally heard Amir cry for the first time. As doctors rushed the baby to the NICU, Prince followed behind them with sheer terror crackling across his face! I looked on in horror, wishing there was something I could do. With no other option, I called my mom. We wept, and prayed, searching for answers that didn't seem to exist. Meanwhile, Prince stayed by his son's side while another team moved fever-ishly to stabilize Mayte.

Amir went through numerous surgeries that even a muscle-bound, grown man, would have trouble enduring! It was difficult to watch. One afternoon, when Prince had come home to shower, change, and get his hair done, he mentioned that he didn't know how Mayte stayed so strong.

"A mother's love can lift the car off a child, move bricks from buildings, and pulls stars out of the sky, if need be!" I said.

Prince laughed. "I've never felt that type of love. I'm glad my son has her." He dropped his smile and he let out a deep sigh, adding, "I'm so tired."

I nodded. "It's times like these that we have to rely on God's strength. Not ours!" And we went to the word of God.

We were in the salon, and I grabbed the Bible that I always kept nearby. First, I turned to Isaiah 40:29 *He gives strength to the weary, and increases the power of the weak!*

Then I flipped to Psalms 27:14 *Wait on the Lord; be of good courage and he shall strengthen your heart; wait, I say, on the Lord.*

Finally, I went to Psalms 91:1: *Those who live in the shelter of the Most High will find rest in the shadow of the Almighty.*

Prince and I prayed for God's strength through this test, and we thanked Him for peace. After I finished cleaning up, Prince signaled that it was time to head back to the hospital, and he wanted me to go with him. Needless to say, everything else at Paisley was still business as usual. It was just me and Prince with the security team, rollin' back-and-forth, believing for a breakthrough.

Days had passed, along with many operations, when doctors told Prince and Mayte that a trach would have to be inserted in Amir's throat to help him breathe. I told Prince that my brother Pete had to have a tracheotomy during his battle with Guillain-Barré syndrome, and that he kept snatching it out of his throat.

"Quit making me laugh when I'm trying to be serious!" Prince, said elbowing me. Then, with his tone more serious, he said, "It's crazy how our lives are so similar."

"That's because God don't make no mistakes."

"Yeah, you're right about that."

Prince stood in silence for a while, as if contemplating his own words. Finally, he said, "Amir's organs are shutting down one by one, and no one deserves to live like that."

The doctor explained to Prince and Mayte that if they didn't have the tracheotomy done, they were essentially letting baby Amir go. I know Prince loved his son with his whole heart, but I could also see the pain in his eyes when he looked down at that baby, who was bone of his bone and flesh of his flesh, but yet so broken. Prince was one of the most talented and powerful men in the entertainment industry, and for the first time he was witnessing a situation he couldn't fix. This wasn't like being disrespected by Warner Brothers, and then changing his name to bypass the system. There was no recourse for Amir! And, no way to remedy what wasn't quite right!

The whole scene was completely overwhelming! I ran out to the hallway to call my mom, and I spoke to her between sobs. "I don't understand!" I cried. "It's too much!"

My mother's response was the same as it always was no matter what the crisis. I closed my eyes as she said, softly, "Just pray, baby." We'd prayed throughout the pregnancy, then we prayed a little harder once Mayte was put on bed rest. We prayed harder still after Amir was born and diagnosed. And that day we sent up our most fervent prayers yet! Asking God for a miraculous healing! But Amir's future had already been decided, and God was already calling him home.

I walked back toward the hospital room, and saw Prince gently kiss Mayte on her forehead, just as if he were about to run to the grocery store to grab some ice cream. Then he turned to me and said "Let's go, Kim."

I looked over at Mayte and saw the pain of losing her baby swell into confusion and then anger that her husband would leave right in the middle of it. Our eyes connected. And as a woman, I could read the thoughts of her mind without her even uttering a word. But Prince said we had to leave, so I left.

I always arrived before Prince at the airport so I could make sure his luggage was accounted for. I held it together for as long as I could in front of Prince, but when I got to the airport, I broke down in sobs! I felt crushed by the agony of Amir's death and short life! Even then, in the midst of grief, I knew that there were no wasted experiences and that Amir's life served a purpose! Both Prince and Mayte were forever changed! They were changed in ways that I could never fully understand. Hours later, we were off to Miami - Prince, his bodyguard, and me. Prince had never dealt with heartache well, and this time was no exception. He reverted back to his old self, to the Prince he was, before Amir, and before Mayte came and stole his heart.

> *"If U ask God 2 love U longer*
> *Every breath U take*
> *Will make U stronger"*[25]
>
> **—From the song "The Holy River" by Prince**

Prince just needed to "be," and I didn't try to get in the way of that. He wanted to go out constantly, to the movies, and to clubs. Yet, even as he tried to fade into the booming bass of the speakers and the mass of bodies swaying back and forth, he never stood out more, never looked lonelier in a room full of people. I traveled with him as a silent companion while he worked through things the only way he knew how, hiding behind his dark shades, and refusing to speak about his child or his wife.

When we were back in Chanhassen weeks later, riding around town, I heard a strange clanking sound coming from the backseat where Prince was sitting. I turned around and saw him pick up the urn with Amir's ashes, clutching it to his chest like it was his most prized possession. Our eyes met, but he looked away without saying anything, and I knew not to ask. People grieve in strange ways, my mother said. And that was Prince's way. He carried around Amir's ashes for months on end, until one day, he didn't need to anymore. But even as Prince was starting to move past the pain, he still didn't want to let the public know about Amir's death, or his condition. He couldn't keep it quiet for long, though. When Prince discovered how the information got out to the tabloids, to Oprah, and to the rest of the world, Prince's world got much darker before the sun rose again.

Here's the funny thing about Prince. He never really respected most women in his life. Yet, he ended up giving the ones closest to him a lot of power. Definitely more power than they should have had! I tried to warn him every time, of course. But sometimes men have to learn things the hard way.

Arlene and Erlene Mojica were twin sisters and friends of Mayte. Mayte got them both jobs at Paisley—one was hired before Amir's birth to be his nanny. The other ended up working as a bodyguard, and signing our checks. It was an immediate red flag, to me, that Prince would hand over information about his bank accounts and other personal files to someone he didn't know just because she was Mayte's friend! On top of that, I had walked into Arlene's apartment and seen her chanting over a table full of candles surrounding a doll that was as black as night! I asked Arlene what the hell was going on! I told her it looked like she was practicing voodoo, and said that if she was up to anything crazy, it was going to be her ass! Arlene denied any wrongdoing, and said that she was Catholic, and praying for Prince's soul after Amir's death. She claimed that she was sent to protect Prince, but I didn't believe it for a second! Her pitiful explanation was all I needed for every single alarm in my brain to start ringing at full blast!

I stood in the position of the hairstylist, and I had nothing to do with Mayte's entourage, but I definitely knew that Arlene was doing the devil's work!

I told Prince about what I saw, but I didn't hold my breath waiting on him to do anything about it. I knew he wouldn't want me snitching, nor would he want to believe that Mayte was responsible for bringing some mess like that into his life. But for some reason, he listened to me.

Maya Angelou said, "When people show you who they are the first time, believe them." Arlene had nailed her coffin shut, as my dad would say, and all of the antics to follow only dug her grave even deeper!

Prince heard that there were rumors swirling, that Arlene was trying to sell a story to the press claiming that Prince was responsible for Amir's death! If it had been me, I would have cussed her out and shown her the door! But, Prince kept it cool, and called Arlene into a meeting in his office. They talked for a while, and their interactions seemed to be proceeding as normal, like maybe Prince wasn't going to say anything after all. But then, when Arlene stood to leave, something fell out of her purse.

It was a mini tape recorder! The physical proof that every rumor was true!

As it turned out, the woman who Mayte was going to entrust with the care of her family had been secretly recording conversations between her and Prince! Including those that took place at the hospital before, and after, Amir's death.

Arlene was probably planning to sell the tapes for a lot of money. But, since she'd been caught, the next best plan was to run to the tabloids! And, she headed straight to the *Enquirer*. She told them that Amir didn't die of natural causes but that he had died because Prince ignored the doctor's wishes and took the baby home. Where, according to Arlene's ridiculous story, Amir died in *her* arms.

Prince was able to stop the story from running. Only, by offering to pay her *double* what the paper would! Unfortunately, enough people had heard the claims—and the claims were serious enough—that the county authorities had to launch an investigation. It was all easily refuted, once the hospital confirmed that Prince did nothing to jeopardize Amir's health! The doctors had been by his side when the baby died; and, most importantly, Arlene had been nowhere around.

Prince responded to Arlene's fool claims by suing her for libel and breach of contract, since she had signed a confidentiality agreement. The damage had been done, though, and it was irreparable. Prince was far too private to get past such a major violation of his trust, and adding that to Amir's death was just too much.

> *"They don't care where they kick U,*
> *Just as long as they hurt U"*[26]
>
> —From the song "Thieves in the Temple" by Prince

After we returned from Miami, we all kind of tiptoed around Paisley. No one wanting to trigger Prince, or Mayte, or remind them about what happened. Everything with them was business as usual, though. While I was concerned, I knew the best thing was for me to keep it moving.

"Betcha By Golly Wow" had been recorded while Mayte was pregnant. Despite losing Amir, Prince wanted to push forward with the video shoot. Much to our surprise, he also wanted to keep the original concept. There were ballerinas and lots of children in every scene, and there's a part that shows Prince running into the hospital to meet a "newly pregnant" Mayte. They even filmed the scene in the same hospital where she had just lost her baby. For everyone on the staff and crew, it broke us. But that's showbiz, baby! And the show must go on!

Mayte was the most understanding of anyone, and she was willing to do whatever she thought would work to heal Prince. Prince, and the band, had gone to Chicago several times to shoot live performances at Harpo studios. So, when Oprah announced that she wanted to come to Paisley to have a sit-down with Prince and Mayte, Mayte agreed to that, too.

The day that Oprah was set to arrive, Prince and I hit the salon as usual, with Prince blaring "Soft and Wet" from his CD player. We danced along as I got him shampooed and styled; making sure that there was not a hair out of place for the cameras. He looked in the mirror, ran his fingers along his sideburns, and said, "Show time baby!!" Mayte, on the other hand, was fresh out of the hospital after being treated for an infection, and Lord knows she was still reeling from Amir's death. But she was still expected to show up and show out.

Prince took Oprah on a tour of the facility while Mayte was being prepped in hair and makeup. Oprah was amazed at how huge the compound was, and when she said that Harpo Studios could fit inside of Paisley Park, we all gasped in disbelief! She put a few of us on camera, including me, and when I sat down to talk to her, she wanted to know what I called him, since this was still the "Artist Formerly Known As Prince" era.

"I just call him sir," I replied. "Most of the time I don't have to call him anything because he's watching you all the time, if you're in the room with him, anyway! And if he's not paying attention, I cough when I enter the room, or knock something over. Whatever it takes to get the job done and get his attention."

Oprah cracked up laughing!

Soon after, we all gathered in the atrium to witness the taping of the most highly anticipated interview of the year.

First, Oprah quizzed him about "Sex in the Summer," the song he wrote featuring Amir's heartbeat.

Prince beatboxed the rhythm and said, "Yep, that's the baby."

The discussion then moved to the round building next to Paisley. That was where the playground was built, and inside was a fabulous nursery that Mayte hadn't even seen yet. Prince told Oprah it was his favorite room for the children to come to.

She tried to catch him up in his words. "Do you mean the child in you? Or the children to come?"

"The children," he said.

"Well it's been rumored the baby boy was born with birth defects."

"It's all good," Prince said, not missing a beat. "Never mind what you hear."

Oprah wasn't fazed either. "What's the status of the baby?"

"Our family exists; we're just beginning."

All of us in the background cringed with fear and held our breath, waiting to hear if she would keep pushing, keep trying to get more information. Prince kept it together magnificently, though, and Mayte just sat there smiling sheepishly. She had been instructed to say nothing about Amir, and she passed her test with flying colors.

Next, Oprah asked how they met, and Prince responded that he'd told Rosie Gaines, "That's my wife right there," as soon as he saw her.

We all knew the truth, including Mayte, and I could see her shifting in her seat, trying not to look Oprah in the eyes. Prince, meanwhile, was just as bold and as arrogant as could be.

It was painful to watch as he reached his arm around Mayte's back and pressed it there, as if to say, "That's the story and don't you change it."

When Prince talked about his and Mayte's past lives and how he felt that she was a sister or maybe even his wife in another life, Oprah turned to Mayte. "Isn't that weird?"

I wanted to shout right then, "Lady, you don't know the half of it." But, truthfully, it wasn't weird anymore. We had all been around Prince so long; it was all very normal to us!

Not long afterward, Prince came over to the kitchen for touchups, and poor Mayte tore out of there so quick no one had time to say a word to her!

"How was that?" he asked, while I fixed his hair.

All I could do was shake my head. "Painful."

Maybe he didn't hear me, or maybe he only wanted to believe the narrative in his mind, but he shook his head, in disagreement, and then went into the Muhammad Ali shuffle. "I'm the greatest," he said. "I'm the greatest!"

I waited for him to calm down, to stop being silly, and I put my hands gently on his shoulders. "You good?"

"As soon as I restore peace to my kingdom and get all these folks out of my house, I will be," he said. He started laughing then, as he walked off to go shoot the B-roll for the show.

I honestly think that if the baby had been healthy, Prince and Mayte would have stayed together until the day Prince died. But it wasn't to be.

There are so many more stories that I want to share with you!

Stories about his marriage to Manuela, or traveling around the world with the band, and watching him order every single item on the hotel room service menu only to eat the chocolate chip cookies!!! Or the time he rented a 17- room mansion, but literally, only lived out of two rooms! And then there's a funny story about when we were on the boat in Hawaii!!! And, I will! I will share them. But I just couldn't fit them all in this 1st glimpse behind the purple curtain!

This whole process has been a difficult one for me. It's been a grieving process. Going back through all the memories has been one of the most challenging, yet gratifying journeys I have ever had to take.

It was one of the most challenging; because, not only did I lose my employer, I lost my friend! My brother! We were tight! And it meant having to personally face the fact that he was really gone! I didn't want to admit that to myself for a long time.

It became one of the most gratifying; because, in the process of remembering, I got to see his smile again, and I got to hear his laugh, and remember his playfulness once more. And it was then I realized that I could share something of his life that only few got to see! Who he really was! And in the process I also got to meet so many of you! I felt your love, and your love for him, in everything we did to get this message out, and into your hands!

But, more than anything, if there was one thing that I could get you to take away from this peek behind the purple curtain, it would be simply this: Prince was a man made of flesh and blood. If he was cut, he would bleed red just like the rest of us! Most importantly, he did not want to be idolized. He was a musical genius, a lover, a businessman, a husband, a father and a humanitarian. Yes! But all he ever wanted to be was, normal.

He knew he was different. He knew he was special. But, in his mind he was just like you and me. He had struggles. He had success. He was not perfect!!! And, he had flaws! But, unlike you and me, he lived life out loud, on a grander stage.

LOVE 2 THE 9'S

Andrea Williams
(andreawilliams615@gmail.com)

> Thank you for bringing these words to life.

Photographer, Designer and Artists:

Randee St. Nicholas - Photographer

Debbie McGuan – Designer/Artist

Ashley Byrd - Photographer

www.ansphoto.com

Moises Suriel - Artist

(moisessuriel@gmail.com)

Gary Card - Artist

(garycard@gmail.com)

Book Cover Artwork

Germancreative

Formatting

Glenn@Sarco Press

www.sarcopress.com

Graphic Design

GiGi Bill

> Your artwork enhanced my stories.
> Thank you for your visual gifts.

THE BEAUTIFUL ONES...
CASUAL CONVERSATION

To be Prince's personal hairstylist says so much about you. You had to be at the top of your game and very confident in who you are to not be intimidated by Prince. Do you credit how you were raised for your confidence and work ethic?

Absolutely. My daddy taught me that success is when opportunity meets preparedness, and my mom taught me to always walk in my purpose. I wasn't intimidated because I was never that star struck.

I would imagine that Prince was surrounded by people who told him what he wanted to hear. Were you one of the few people who could be honest with Prince?

I was honest to a fault, and I got sent to time out quite a bit. But integrity is a must.

Did Prince have any idea how much he/his music are loved?

He absolutely knew, and he reciprocated the love nightly on stage.

I've experienced Prince live 16 times, but when Prince performed 21 nights at The Forum, so many people got to experience Prince live for the first time! Was it as special for Prince as it was for us in Los Angeles?

Prince was on a mission to save The Forum for Dr. Ulmer. No other artist has given his or her time and talent like him.

Prince's music has gotten me through some rough times. Did you help Prince get through his rough times, and did he help you as well?

We laughed, cried, and prayed together. Iron sharpens iron.

... Deidra Blanton on Hawthorne, CA

Did you and Prince ever give each other nicknames?

Prince had multiple personalities, and I called his mean entity "Hollywood." Everyone stayed away from him.

If any, which season or time of year did Prince enjoy the most?

I noticed that we always went back to Minnesota during winter and the holiday season. Traveling with him was my first experience seeing the seasons change.

Did Prince ever talk to you about us (his fans), and what did he say that would bring us joy and appreciation?

He knew that he was a vessel used by God to bring joy to the world through music. He has connected souls all over the world through Love 4 One Another.

Did you ever join Prince in his place of worship?

I went to Kingdom Hall regularly with Prince.

What were Prince's most profound words ever expressed to you that showed his gratitude for having you in his life? What was your response and how did you feel?

The long days and nights often seemed unrewarded, but he would thank me for being there, and he told me that my presence was required. He just wanted to be "normal," but the bar was too high.

… Elleatrice Thompson of New York, NY

Did Prince ever work on music or write songs while you were doing his hair?

Always. He said his gift was a blessing and a curse.

Later in his career, when Prince began wearing an afro/bush, did you style it for him, or did he handle it himself?

Yes, I maintained it. He couldn't take care of it alone.

Did you watch Prince's concerts from the sidelines to see how his hair was holding up, or did you wait backstage to assess his hair?

Both. I stood on the side of the stage to watch the brilliance in artistry. Backstage was when I touched him up and cleaned him up.

You once mentioned that you sang backup on one of Prince's songs ("Freaks on the Side"). How did he approach you when he asked you to participate?

We were in the salon after his hair service, and he looked at me and said, "I need your voice!" I told him I couldn't sing, but he told me he could make my voice sound like whatever he wanted.

My favorite hair on Prince was during the Batman and Graffiti Bridge eras. What was your favorite style for him?

That's like choosing your favorite child, but if I had to pick, I would say the short hair for the *Ebony* cover.

... Sharon E. Carter of Glenarden, MD

What was the most fun you had with Prince?

In the hair salon bagging on each other and watching comedy shows.

When were you most disappointed by Prince?

When he fired people without notice.

What is the biggest change you witnessed in Prince during the time you worked for him?

The shift when Amir was about to be born. He was a kinder, gentler individual.

What is something Prince told you (or advice he's given you) that you will never forget?

Don't allow other people to make you angry. When you're upset, the body releases a toxin that causes deadly heart rhythms, and you should never give someone that much power over you.

If you could see Prince one more time, what would you want to say to him?

Is heaven as glorious as they say it is?

... Jacqueline Fair of Houston, TX

Was Prince able to record music with his Dad and Mom together with him? If so, what was the name of the song?

"Father Song." John Nelson wrote the melody and Prince played piano.

Did he get a chance to draft a children's script for a movie?

No.

Did Prince have plans to/did he record a children's album?

Not to my knowledge.

Who would you recommend to complete his autobiography, "The Beautiful Ones"?

Spike Lee or Tavis Smiley.

… Alice O'Brien of Norfolk, VA

You have said in interviews that you and Prince have cried together. For what reasons did Prince cry?

Times of sorrow, including the death of Amir, as well as both of his parents.

You have seen Prince with many women, but who do you think was his soulmate?

Mayte.

I know Prince was behind many donations and acts of kindness. What are some that really stand out or that affected you personally?

Computer lab for Los Angeles children, HIV testing and breast cancer screenings, support for the Black Lives Matter movement, paying for the funeral services of young men, centers to teach coding and urban farmers, the Feed My Starving Children organization.

Because of the many years you spent with Prince and the closeness you had with him, I think you know him better than most. What do you think he would say was his biggest regret?

That he didn't have children.

... Margaret (Maggie) Sporcic of Chesaning, MI

THE LOVESEXY SANCTUARY

A SPECIAL "THANK YOU" to everyone listed here. Because of you and your love for Prince, you help keep his legacy alive in this book. You're now an eternal part of Prince's story.

THE DIAMONDS N CURLZ EXPERIENCE

Tania Capree	Los Angeles	California
Jacqueline Flair	Houston	Texas

THE DIAMOND EXPERIENCE

Wanda Pillai	Maricopa	Arizona

THE PURPLE EXPERIENCE

Karen Higginbotham	Alpharetta	Georgia
Ellece McKinley	Bloomfield Hills	Michigan

THE GOLD EXPERIENCE

Alice O'Brien	Norfolk	Virginia
Deidra W. Blanton	Hawthorne	California
Sharon E. Carter	Glenarden	Maryland
Nadine Rivers Johnson	Stone Mountain	Georgia

Margaret Sporcic	Chesaning	Michigan
Gail McMullen	Santa Barbara	California
Elleatrice Thompson	New York	New York
Dawn T. Pernell	Williamstown	New Jersey
Carrie Bernhardt	El Dorado	Kansas
Clare Rountree	Honolulu	Hawaii

THE SILVER EXPERIENCE

Dominica Soliz of DomSol Henna	Houston	Texas
Craig, Crystal Alexander & Family	Fresno	Texas
Eric and Amber Rogers	Winchester	Kentucky
Catherine Eddy	Healesville	Australia
Karen Surmiak	Melbourne Victoria	Australia
Kamie S. Keck	Richmond	Virginia
Sherry DiMauro	Stratford	Connecticut
Kimberly A. Hankins	Seabrook	Maryland
Jeanne Mulholland	Newport	Kentucky
Audrey Johnson	Ellicott City	Maryland
Gloria J. Tava	St. Paul	Minnesota
KaNisa Williams	Atlanta	Georgia
Inou Lovett	Macon	Georgia
Renie Micheale	Bismarck	North Dakota
Nick Garcia	San Angelo	Texas
Mi-Ling Stone Poole	Edmond	Oklahoma
Lisa Davis	New York	New York
Shannon Snider	Los Angeles	California
Ana Holcombe	Fayettville	North Carolina

THE PAISLEY EXPERIENCE

Kim Trip	Portland	Oregon
Patricia Geishirt	Deerfield	Wisconsin
Nova Lea A. Bradshaw	Farmington	Missouri
Lisa Carter-Chunuwe	Chicago	Illinois
Tia W. Stasko	New Orleans	Louisiana
Lisa Alves	Lorton	Virginia
Barbara Robertson	Jackson	Mississippi
The Purple Army	Los Angeles	California
Carolyn Ross	Bridgeville	Pennsylvania
Aisha Sims	Margate	Florida
Natalie Antonia Borg	London	England
Pamela Kiefert	Miami	Florida
Amanda Ohira	Raleigh	North Carolina
Doris Gaylord	Elgin	Illinois
Craig and Crystal Alexander	Fresno	Texas
Traci Humphrey	Jamaica	New York
Omna Alexander	Vallejo	California
Monica Dick	Indianapolis	Indiana
Jean Renee Nukala	Angora	Minnesota
Portia Chinnery	Saddle Brook	New Jersey
Floyd El-Dred	Northampton	United Kingdom
Sharon R. Gaines	Lithonia	Georgia
Ruby Brandenburg	Ocean Shores	Washington
Angela Roberts	Cordova	Tennessee
Deon Marcelin-Jackson	Apple Valley	California
Meghan Hernandez	Ventura	California
Maefe L. Nunez	Seattle	Washington
Amy Austin	Naples	Florida
Andrea L. Mitchell	Oakbrook Terrace	Illinois

Jeanne-Michele Salander	San Jose	California
Detrice M. Wallace	Broadlands	Virginia
Tiffany Dugar Hatchett	Houston	Texas
Silvana Peters	Dusseldorf	Germany
Rene P. Davis	Lanham	Maryland
Sharon Baldwin	Houston	Texas
Sylvan Lumsden	Duvall	Washington
Dawna Twyman	Martinsburg	West Virginia
Delaine Peplinski	Kalamazoo	Michigan
Keirra L. Dillard	Hampton	Virginia
Skylar Scurlock	Memphis	Tennessee
Tanisha Curtis	Redondo Beach	California
Denise M. Hilton	Millerton	New York
Kirk Carman	Troy	Michigan

THE PAISLEY EXPERIENCE

Koquise Tyson	Concord	California
Deborah Lee Davis	Ambler	Pennsylvania
Gailya Goode	Lancaster	California
Iva Andrea Grossovai	Prague	Czech Republic
Erin Tripp	Costa Mesa	California
Linda Carfagno	Middletown	New Jersey
Carol Blaubach	Raton	New Mexico
Alisa Joseph	Charlotte	North Carolina
Annette Carpenter	Talbott	Tennessee
Danita Wallace Ealy	Sugar Land	Texas
Mona Austin	Blue Springs	Missouri
Deb Harvey	Bayswater North	Australia

THE LOVE EXPERIENCE

Dianne Seymore	Macomb	Illinois
Devin N. Haley	Bellwood	Illinois
Matt Osgood	St. Albans	United Kingdom
Paul Kirk	Keighley	United Kingdom
Angela Reardon	Alabaster	Alabama
Gwen Pitzen	Oregon	Ohio
Maureen O. Sullivan and Mark O'Connor	London	United Kingdom
Krystal Banaszewski	West St. Paul	Minnesota
Dom Puglisi	Greystanes NSW	Australia
Jamie A. Shaffer	Scranton	Pennsylvania
Michael Robertson	Wichita	Kansas
Lynne Valento	Oakdale	Minnesota
Kathryn Redsky	Brown Deer	Wisconsin
Sharad Patel	Richmond	Virginia
Cheryl Beato	Houston	Texas
Diana Romano	Northampton	Pennsylvania
Amy Taylor	Toledo	Ohio
Kathy Valenzuela	Fresno	California
Kyla Holcombe-Scott	Fayetteville	North Carolina
Nadine Conner	Cedar Rapids	Iowa
Khris Gaines	Los Angeles	California
Jan L. Burt	Wichita	Kansas
B.S.	Goose Creek	South Carolina
Gina Kennon	Charleston	South Carolina
Barbara Rogers	Deerfield Beach	Florida
Tara McCollum	Hoover	Alabama
Deborah Dorsam	Peru	Indiana
Monique Vanessa Wheeler	Lubbock	Texas
Tifany Shelby	Rosenberg	Texas

THE LOVE EXPERIENCE

David Gibbons	Southport	United Kingdom
Benjamin Bradley Jr.	Jackson	Mississippi
Marcia Terlau	Erlanger	Kentucky
Lisa Jones-Pitts	Mobile	Alabama
Pamela Kiefert	Miami	Florida
Marilyn Thurman	Lubbock	Texas
Kim Ina	Houston	Texas
Cheryl A. Rosa	Providence	Rhode Island
Tracey Blackmon	Philadelphia	Pennsylvania
Candida King	Milwaukee	Wisconsin
Bonnie Jenkins	Woodbridge	Virginia
Annik Dupaty	Madison	Wisconsin
Paul Cooper	Perth	Australia
Olga Hernandez	Ventura	California
Bonnie (Bon Val) Valens	Tacoma	Washington
Mojo Bass	Deerfield Beach	Florida
Diane Tigner	Lima	Ohio
Tami Neubauer Foster	Burnsville	Minnesota
Tony Kennedy	London	England
Kirk Carman	Troy	Michigan
Kirk Carman	Troy	Michigan
Jenna DeFrancesco	Escondido	California
Ole Rensen	Aarhus	Denmark
Jeannette Brock	San Pedro	California
Jennifer Michlitsch	Little Canada	Minnesota
Sissel Baade Bie	Stavanger	Norway
Julie Stahl	St. Louis	Missouri
JoAnn O. Ramon	Cedar Park	Texas
Rob Staples	London	United Kingdom
Lisa Truax	Winona	Minnesota

Curtis Silas	Inglewood	California
Jennifer R. McVier	Washington	District of Columbia
Lisa and Madison Lincoln	Massillon	Ohio
Carolyn Ross	Bridgeville	Pennsylvania
Ginade Masi	Los Angeles	California

U MAKE MY SUN SHINE

THIS BOOK WOULD not have been possible without God's Divine plan and the orchestration of beautiful people into my life. Chief among those introductions are the men I'm honored to call my manager, mentors, and friends, Darrell Muhammad, Reginald Keith and Arnold Turner. Talk about iron sharpening iron, smoothing out the rough edges… God had you about-face and turn back to the Sun to find me and help bring this book to fruition. Obedience is greater than sacrifice.

I'm grateful to my Stars in the Universe: Sieara, Daphne, Kristen D., Kristen P., Serena, Shakilah, Alyssa, Sydney, and Oriana, my "Delone Beauties," you've allowed me to fulfill my dream of being a Mother. Each of you are Galaxy yet to be fully revealed, and I look forward to watching as you discover what your father LaVel and I have always known, for you to manifest every good and perfect gift God has placed inside you. Ms. Phyllis thank you for being the best mother-n-love a girl could ever have. Thanks to the entire Delone-Rogers family.

To my parents who shielded, protected, and continue to guide me through adulthood: Thank you for imprinting your love on my heart.

To them Berry Boys, Kenneth, Frank, Pete, and Will: You ride for your sister, peel a cap for you sister. None of this would have been possible without the lessons we learned while growing up together. To the entire Berry lineage I stand on your shoulders. I hope I've made you proud.

To my E.C.M Family, Pastor Shep and Dr. Shalonda Crawford: Thanks 4 bringing the Bible to life and for rocking outside the box but in the WORD. #YallGiveMeLife

Bishop W.T. and Kimberly Ervin, your prayers got us through.

To my Trues, Jenique, Cosetta, Lil Rosie, Keisha, Sabrina, Marna, Brownie, Alicia, Zenora, Leslie, Lesley, and T.J. To Monique for holding down the home fort. To D.L.C and My Girlfriends Network: You all make amazing family members.

To my Sistaz/Prayer Warriors and executive assistants, Tamara Parnell and Tia Weber Stasko: Thanks for keeping me sane and being my rock when I wanted to run and hide; you stood tall on the WORD.

Ms. Sharon Baldwin: Thanks for taking a chance on my mission and dedicating time to understand my authentic delivery.

Last but certainly not least—To everyone who stopped me in the grocery store or airport, who came to hear me speak or left a comment on my page: You rock!! Thank you for being the best part of *Diamonds and Curlz.* I appreciate your patience with me as I grew throughout this process.

To everyone: Thanks for coming along for the ride; you won't be disappointed. And as

Prince used to say…

Hold on2 yo WIGZ!

HAVE A HEART

KIM BERRY IS an elite hairstylist based in Los Angeles. Following her formal education at Pacific Beauty College, the universe aligned her path to cross with that of rock royalty Prince, kick starting a whirlwind education of 29 years at the "University of Prince Rogers Nelson."

For nearly three decades, Kim saw Prince at his most vulnerable times, witnessing what few others did and serving as a constant presence through many of the ups and downs of his career. Others came and went over the years, but Kim was blessed to roll with Prince almost longer than anyone else. She may have started as his hairstylist, but she ended up as family.

Kim's work with Prince has been seen all over the world and featured in the pages of the most prestigious fashion and music publications, including *Vogue*, *W*, *Allure*, and *Rolling Stone*, just to name a few. Kim has collaborated with esteemed fashion photographers Patrick De Marchellier, David La Chapelle, and Randee St.Nicholas. She has also delivered her services for some of Prince's most indelible live performances, including the *1999* concert, his 2004 induction into the Rock & Roll Hall of Fame, and the 2007 Super Bowl Half Time performance, as well as multiple tours, album covers, and videos.

In addition to Prince, Kim has worked alongside many other members of Hollywood's elite, including Katt Williams, Nicole Ari Parker, Yolanda "Yo Yo" Whitaker, Naturi Naughton,

Loretta Devine, Wendy Raquel Robinson, Ne-Yo, David Tutera, and many more.

After returning from Egypt, where she competed with the Moehair International styling team in a hair battle with other platform artists, Kim was named "National Artistic Director" for the 3Deluxe color line of Milan, Italy. The announcement was made by Gina Rivera, owner of Phenix Salon and Suites and featured entrepreneur on the hit TV show "Undercover Boss."

Being a living example in this purpose-driven life is incredibly important to Kim, and she believes that giving back is a must. Her salon was known for organizing HIV and breast cancer awareness days for the community, while also organizing mammogram screenings, feeding and clothing the homeless, and facilitating welfare-to-work makeover programs. Kim recently teamed with "Dress for Success" in Houston, Texas, to continue those efforts.

As a mother, daughter, businesswoman, influencer, philan-thropist and God Chick who balances career, ministry, and family—all while turning her Passion into Purpose—Kim's goal is to empower young people to live their best versions of themselves. She currently serves on the board of the Youth Drama Theater Corporation, which provides at-risk, inner-city youth with performing arts, tutoring, and mentor/scholarship programs in L.A.

TO CONTACT THE AUTHOR:
KIM BERRY

www.diamondsncurlz.com

Media Inquiries:

Media@KimBOnSet.com

Speaking & Appearances:

Booking@KimBOnSet.com

Facebook:

Kim B On Set

Instagram:

kimbonset2

Twitter:

@kimbonset

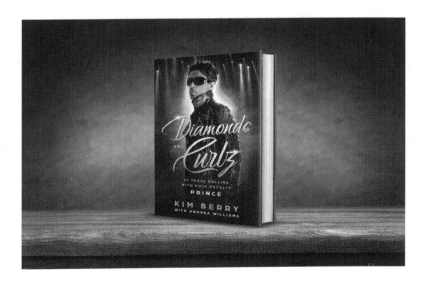

REFLECTION

1. **"Despite everything, no one can dictate who you are to other people."**

   CBS Minnesota, April 21, 2016, Minnesota. cbslocal.com Page 3.

2. **"A strong spirit transcends rules."**

   Brainy Quote>quotes>prince_450412. Page 3.

3. **"A Promise 2 see Jesus in the morning light"**

   Nelson, Prince Rogers. "Thunder." *Diamonds and Pearls,* October 1, 1991, track 1, Paisley Park Records and Warner Bros. Records, Page 15.

4. **"It's ok to fear the answers, but you can't avoid them. They are training ground for the process."**

   A Wrinkle in Time. Directed by Ava DuVernay, Walt Disney Pictures, 2018. Page 19.

5. **"Blow that devil away"**

   Nelson, Prince Rogers. "Eye No." *Lovesexy,* May 10, 1988, track 1, Warner Bros. Records Inc. Page 21.

6. **"I alone cannot change the world, but I can carry a stone across the water to create many ripples"**

Mother Teresa, www.goodreads.com. Page 26.

7. **"4 U Eye shall B wild"**

Nelson, Prince Rogers. "Anna Stesia." *Lovesexy*, May 10, 1988, track 4, Paisley Park Records and Warner Bros. Records Inc. Page 35.

8. **"Don't wait for opportunities to come to you, create your own"**

Mr. Donald Berry, 1970. Page 44.

9. **"Success is when preparedness meets opportunity. So when the opportunity presents itself, will you be prepared?"**

Mr. Donald Berry, 1989. Page 47.

10. **"Prince was a diamond of matchless beauty, that everywhere light struck him, a color emitted from his being"**

A tribute from Minister Louis Farrakhan, *Prince – The Essence of Beauty*, April 26, 2016. Page 54.

11. **"It's all good when U know the only fame Is the light that comes from God & the joy U get 2 say His name"**

Nelson, Prince Rogers. "Don't Play Me." *Crystal Ball*, January 29, 1998, track 2, *The Truth*, NPG Records. Page 62.

12. **"I'll show you fat meat is greasy"**

Mr. Donald Berry, 1993. Page 64.

13. **"It is during our darkest moments that we must focus to see the light"**

Aristotle Onassis, www.brainyquote.com, date unknown. Page 76.

14. **"You can depend on God to see you through, and you can depend on me to pray for you"**

Morton, Bishop Paul S. "Be Blessed." *Memorable Moment,* March 2, 2010, track 6, Light Records. Page 79.

15. **"Think big thoughts. But relish small things."**

Jackson Brown, Jr., www.goodreads.com, *Life's Little Instruction Book,* November 4, 2002 by Element (first published 1991), ISBN 0007145179 (ISBN 13: 9780007145171). Page 92.

16. **"I had crossed the line, I was free; but, there was no one to welcome me to the land of freedom. I was a stranger in a strange land."**

Harriet Tubman, en.m.wikiquote.org, date unknown. Page 99.

17. **Excerpts from an Online Letter from The Artist. 1996.**

https://www.businessinsider.com/prince-secret-letter-2016-5 Page 105.

18. **"Without God It's just the blind Leading the blind"**

Nelson, Prince Rogers. "Colonized Mind." *Lotusflow3r/ MPLSound*, March 29, 2009, track 5, NPG Records. Page 108.

19. "Freedom lies in being bold"

Robert Frost, NBC News, Bela Kornizer, November 23, 1952, Video Documentary, *A Conversation with Robert Frost (1952).* Page 110.

20. "We are warriors who serve Good and Light in the Universe Sometimes we rescue; sometimes we guide"

A Wrinkle in Time. Directed by Ava DuVernay, Walt Disney Pictures, 2018. Page 111.

21. "Until the end of time, I'll B There 4 U U own my heart N mind Eye truly adore U"

Nelson, Prince Rogers. "Adore." *Sign O' the Times,* March 30, 1987, track 16, Paisley Park Records, Warner Bros. Inc. Page 124.

22. "Meet me in another world, space and joy"

Nelson, Prince Rogers. "Girls & Boys." *Parade,* March 31, 1986, track 5, Paisley Park Records and Warner Bros. Records. Page 128.

23. "How could Eye 4get that U R the RULE U R my God I am your child"

Nelson, Prince Rogers. "Anna Stesia." *Lovesexy,* May 10, 1988, track 4, Paisley Park Records and Warner Bros. Inc. Page 141.

24. "When something on the inside of you connects with what's happening outside of you, it's a sign that a portion of your life is a part of the solution."

Sarah Jakes Roberts, *don't settle for safe,* Thomas Nelson publisher, April 18, 2017, ISBN-10 071809588X. Page 143.

25. **"If U ask God 2 love U longer Every breath U take Will make U stronger"**

Nelson, Prince Rogers. "The Holy River." *Emancipation*, November 19, 1996, track 8, Disc 2, NPG Records and EMI Records. Page 147.

26. **"They don't care where they kick U, Just as long as they hurt U"**

Nelson, Prince Rogers. "Thieves in the Temple." *Graffiti Bridge*, August 21, 1990, track 12, Paisley Park Records and Warner Bros. Records. Page 150.

Album, Song and Artist References

Encourage you to listen to not only these songs and albums but Prince's entire catalog

Xtralovable

Prince. *Hit n Run Phase Two*, December 12, 2015, track 6, NPG Records, Page iii.

Somewhere Here On Earth

Prince. *Planet Earth*, July 15, 2007, track 3, NPG Records and Columbia Records, Page v.

Beautiful, Loved and Blessed

Prince (featuring Tamar). *3121,* March 21, 2006, track 10, NPG Records and Universal Music Group, Page v,1.

Revelation

Prince. *Hit n Run Phase Two,* December 12, 2015, track 11, NPG Records, Page v,5,6.

Sometimes It Snows in April

Prince, Wendy Melvoin, and Lisa Coleman. *Parade,* March 31, 1986, track 12, Paisley Park Records and Warner Bros. Records, Page v,13,26.

Endorphinmachine

Prince. *The Gold Experience*, September 26, 1995, track 3, Warner Bros. Records and NPG Records, Page v,51,73,95,117,137.

Love 2 the 9's

Prince. *Love Symbol Album*, October 13, 1992, track 3, Paisley Park Records and Warner Bros. Records, Page v,155.

The Beautiful Ones

Prince. *Purple Rain*, June 25, 1984, track 3, Warner Bros. Records, Page v,157.

The "Lovesexy" Sanctuary

Prince. *Lovesexy*, May 10, 1988, track 4, Paisley Park Records and Warner Bros. Records Inc., Page v,163.

U Make My Sun Shine

Prince. *The Chocolate Invasion*, March 29, 2004, track 10, NPG Records, Page v,171.

Have a Heart

Prince. *One Nite Alone*, May 14, 2002, track 5, NPG Records, Page v,175.

Reflection

Prince. *Musicology*, April 20, 2004, track 12, NPG Records and Columbia Records, Page v,179.

Diamonds and Pearls

Prince. *Diamonds and Pearls*, October 1, 1991, Paisley Park Records and Warner Bros. Records, Page 5,80,127.

Little Red Corvette

Prince. *1999,* October 27, 1982, track 1, Warner Bros. Records, Page 14,47.

1999

Prince. *1999,* October 27, 1982, track 1, Warner Bros. Records, Page 14,47,80.

Purple Rain

Prince. *Purple Rain,* June 25, 1984, Warner Bros. Records, Page 39,47,80,100.

On Bended Knee

Boyz II Men. *II,* August 30, 1994, track10, Motown Records, Page 39.

U Remind Me

Usher. *8701,* August 7, 2001, track 2, Arista Records, Page 39.

Rave Un2 the Joy Fantastic

Prince. *Rave Un2 the Joy Fantastic*, November 2, 1999, New Power Generation Records and Arista Records, Page 53,55.62.

Crystal Ball

Prince. *Crystal Ball*, January 29, 1998, New Power Generation Records, Page 56.

The Vault: Old Friends 4 Sale

Prince. *The Vault: Old Friends 4 Sale,* August 24, 1999, Warner Bros. Records, Page 56.

20Ten

Prince. *20Ten*, July 10, 2010, New Power Generation Records, Page 59.

Batman

Prince. *Batman,* June 20, 1989, Warner Bros. Records, Page 80.

Brown Sugar

D'Angelo. *Brown Sugar,* July 3, 1995, EMI Records, Page 110,111.

Lady

D'Angelo. *Brown Sugar,* July 3, 1995, track 9, EMI Records, Page 111.

Cruisin

D'Angelo. *Brown Sugar,* July 3, 1995, track 7, EMI Records, Page 111.

Area Codes

Ludacris. *Word of Mouf,* November 27, 2001, track 1, Disturbing the Peace and Def Jam South, Page 122,127.

Love Symbol

Prince. *Love Symbol,* October 13, 1992, Paisley Park Records and Warner Bros. Records, Page 127.

3 Chains O' Gold

Direct-to-video film. *3 Chains O' Gold*. Directed by Parris Patton, Randee St. Nicholas and Prince. Produced by Paisley Park. Starring Prince and The New Power Generation.

Music by Prince. Distributed by Warner Music Vision. August 16, 1994, Page 127.

Kamasutra,

Prince. *Kamasutra,* February 14, 1997 (cassette), track 2, January 29, 1998 *Crystal Ball* 5-CD version direct order, March 21, 1998 4-CD version retail stores, Page 134.

The Most Beautiful Girl in the World

Prince. *The Gold Experience,* September 26, 1995, track 7, Warner Bros. Records and NPG Records, Page v,139.

Betcha By Golly Wow

Prince (cover Thom Bell, Linda Creed). *Emancipation,* November 19, 1996, Disc 1, track 6, NPG Records and EMI Records, Page 150.

Soft and Wet

Prince. *For You,* April 7, 1978, track 3, Warner Bros. Records, Page 151.

Sex in the Summer

Prince. *Emancipation,* November 19, 1996, Disc 2, track 1, NPG Records and EMI Records, Page 152.

Made in the USA
Columbia, SC
06 August 2024

39645535R00109